DESCRIPTIVE SYNTAX AND THE ENGLISH VERB

DESCRIPTIVE SYNTAX AND THE ENGLISH VERB

DAVID KILBY

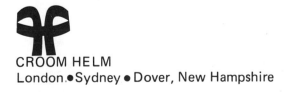

CROOM HELM
London.•Sydney • Dover, New Hampshire

© 1984 David Kilby
Croom Helm Ltd, Provident House, Burrell Row,
Beckenham, Kent BR3 1AT

Croom Helm Australia Pty Ltd, First Floor, 139 King Street,
Sydney, NSW 2001, Australia

British Library Cataloguing in Publication Data

Kilby, David
    Descriptive syntax and the English verb.
    1. English language—Verb 2. English
    language—Syntax
    I. Title
    425   PE1319

    ISBN 0-7099-1544-6
    ISBN 0-7099-1553-5 Pbk

Croom Helm, 51 Washington Street,
Dover, New Hampshire 03820, USA

Library of Congress Catalog Card Number: 84-45287
Cataloging in Publication Data Applied For.

Printed and bound in Great Britain by
Biddles Ltd, Guildford and King's Lynn

CONTENTS

TABLES

ACKNOWLEDGEMENTS

This book has as its basis a course given to postgraduate and undergraduate students at the University of Essex for a number of years. Such virtues as the book has are largely due to the hard work of these students in making it a better course. To all of them I am most grateful. Rod McMillan and I have had long conversations on the subject of chapter 8 which have been very helpful. Jacques Durand has managed to get through the whole book in draft and has made many helpful comments. To these and to all those other colleagues and friends who have provided ideas and encouragement over the years I express my thanks. Of course, the undoubted shortcomings which remain are my problem.

The five tables in chapter 9 and table 10.1 are from <u>Some</u> <u>classes</u> <u>of</u> <u>verbs</u> <u>in</u> <u>English</u> (edited by D. Alexander and W. J. Kunz) and <u>More</u> <u>classes</u> <u>of</u> <u>verbs</u> <u>in</u> <u>English</u> (edited by L. I. Bridgeman, D. Dillinger, C. Higgins, P. D. Seaman and F. A. Shank); both of these are made available through the Indiana University Linguistics Club and the Linguistics Research Project (Principal Investigator F. W. Householder Jr., Assistant Director P. H. Matthews). I am grateful to these bodies for being allowed to reproduce these tables.

INTRODUCTION

This is a book about descriptive grammar, and in particular, about the descriptive grammar of English. The only way in which problems and methods associated with such activity can be illuminated is by trying to do some description, and showing how difficult it can become, and how some of the difficulties can be overcome by using the methods of descriptive linguistics. There are many compendious grammars of English, and books and articles on particular aspects of English grammar, many of them excellent works, useful to students of English and the linguistic investigator alike. But even a brief acquaintance with such works will convince one that they fail to illuminate certain aspects of English, and also contain certain analyses which are unconvincing or inexplicit. If you take seriously the notion of a grammar as a representation of what the speaker of a language knows about his language, then a grammar and a dictionary combined ought to contain all of the information one needs to formulate correct sentences of English and interpret them. But even the largest grammar, and the most informative of dictionaries, will fail such a test. It does not take a great deal of experience of critically reading grammars and dictionaries to discover that an adequate grammar of English would be a very large undertaking indeed. It is not difficult to convince yourself of this: think of a linguistic problem which foreign learners of English stumble on - e.g. the use of the definite article <u>the</u>, or the choice of form of complement sentences as object of some verb. Then look at a large English grammar (e.g. GCE - see section 5 for abbreviations) and a large dictionary (e.g. the OED) to see what they have to say on the problem. It is most unlikely that you will find an adequate account of the problem. Looking at

1

any of the chapters of this book, you will see many problems which are not solved in any existing grammar (or here, for that matter!).

Similarly, there are many excellent works in which English grammar is used as the medium for an exposition of some theory of syntax. It is hardly necessary to say that this is not one of these, but it is, I think, important to note that one consequence of using English or any other single language to exemplify a theory is that the language needs to be simplified somewhat in order for the essential concepts of the theory to be clearly illustrated. It follows that anyone looking at one of these works in a critical frame of mind will be able to find many points of detail which are substantially more complex than is allowed for in such works. More worrying perhaps, one possible result of training budding linguists through such works is that they may begin to believe that such 'laundered' data is in fact the real thing, and this unwittingly encourages the sort of cavalier attitude to data and variability which is characteristic of much of contemporary linguistics. I feel that it is important to add some counterweight to such works, and to encourage an exploratory attitude towards linguistic data. I hope that the present work may be of some use in this respect.

I do not claim to be writing a grammar of English. This is a 'do-it-yourself' book, in the sense that it aims to illustrate what is necessary in the way of data and methods of analysis for you to approach serious problems of English grammar and work towards a solution. There are no definitive solutions here - anyone with the least sense of historical perspective in linguistics should realise that this is in any case an implausible goal - but rather I concentrate on the need to construct alternative possible hypotheses and test the consequences that these hypotheses entail. Just as a grammar is intended (ideally) to show people how to use a language, so in this book the aim is to show people how to go about analysing English (or mutatis mutandis other languages). It will therefore be useful to students of linguistics, to advanced learners of English, and (I hope) to all those fascinated by the complexity of their own language.

The problems of grammar relate to two groups of issues, essentially. Firstly, one has to establish the relevant data; in simple cases this will be totally unproblematic, but there are likely to be areas of grammar where there is variability among speakers, or where vagueness and fuzziness appear to be the rule, or where there is just plain irregularity. There are ways of approaching all of these problems (some of them highly traditional), but it can be said that linguistics has hardly begun to come to grips with the problems raised by reliability of data. The second issue involves permissible areas of explanation. Different linguists react very differently to the problems of what constitutes an explanation; from a fairly eclectic theoretical position, though, it appears that the sorts of factors which one can invoke to account for the existence of certain phenomena do fall into different classes, some relating to the possible nature of a grammar in the traditional sense, others being more akin to functional constraints, while yet others may be historical in nature. I see no reason to exclude any relevant area from consideration here, while recognising that there is much controversy over the issue.

Two factors of a rather more general nature are also relevant to the way in which grammatical problems are approached in this book. The first is that, given that I start from no a priori ideas as to what constitutes an acceptable explanation and description of a phenomenon, the range of hypotheses which are available to me is quite large. (In fact I believe that most linguists really accept many types of explanatory account, but it has become traditional to mask this by suggesting that the range of permissible hypotheses is quite small due to the constraints imposed by linguistic theory.) It therefore seems to be unwise to remain limited to a single hypothesis in dealing with any particular grammatical phenomenon. A useful heuristic in doing descriptive linguistics is to form a number of possible hypotheses about the nature of a phenomenon; it will then be possible to draw out the predictions made by each of these hypotheses, and even if no conclusive result emerges, the method adopted will have led to the consideration of a fairly wide range of facts relevant to the description of the construction. It is not just in linguistics that it is useful to pursue several hypotheses as far as they will go. The second factor is a question of being systematic: perhaps it should not be necessary to say this, but it is important in checking an apparently plausible hypothesis to cross-check and back-check where possible. To take a typical sort of example, if I have looked at a set of data and concluded that all of the verbs which allow a passive variant are of one semantic class, while those

3

which do not allow a passive variant are of another semantic class, it is a relatively simple task to take a random sample of verbs from some source other than the data I have looked at (e.g. a dictionary), to classify them according to this semantic feature, and to test to see if they have a passive variant or not. It is quite surprising to find that many widely-accepted hypotheses in the linguistics literature founder on a relatively simple test of this sort. I have no doubt that the claims I make in subsequent chapters will fall below this sort of standard at a number of points. Indeed, the indeterminacy of data or semantic categorisation often makes this sort of checking difficult or impossible. But it is only by trying to meet standards of explicitness and adequacy that any reasonable descriptive linguistics can result.

It may be that the reader will take away from this book an overwhelming impression of indeterminacy - and this will be because many of the problems involved in describing languages do seem to be indeterminate (at least in the present state of our knowledge). If a problem which arises in the description of language leads us to a nicely structured solution, then any linguist would naturally be delighted, and it would be perverse to argue that it is in any sense preferable to have a more diffuse solution. But in terms of the orientation of contemporary linguistics, the likelihood is rather that neat solutions will be found by 'laundering' the data, and in this perspective it is useful, I think, to redress the balance to some extent by showing that there is much complexity in the patterning of language which cannot be dealt with in such a straightforward way. If linguists are serious in their belief that there is some fundamental regularity inherent in language, the patterns which make up this regularity are surely more likely to be found by facing up to the true complexity of linguistic facts and going beyond them.

0.2. METHODS OF DATA COLLECTION

In order to do linguistics at all we need to have linguistic data to work on, and there is a fairly small range of ways in which we can choose to amass data. When we have such data there are then various things that we can do to it to make it suitable for the sorts of analysis and accounting that we hope to perform on it. For primary data, we can proceed in a number of ways which have different virtues and different limitations:

a. by study of texts, a term commonly understood as referring to literary writing, but used by linguists to refer to all types of language in use, whether written or spoken, literary or everyday, etc. One of the essential properties of texts in linguistic investigation is that they pre-exist (or at least exist independently of) the investigation carried out by the linguist. The text is there for whatever purpose texts may be for, but certainly not merely as a convenient set of data for the linguist to work on. It follows that the major virtue of texts from the linguist's point of view is that of **objectivity** - they can be taken as genuine 'raw data'. Of course, as with all raw data there are problems - people do make linguistic mistakes in writing or speaking, and there are general problems about the need for distinguishing different aspects of style as well as different dialects, etc. And in at least certain fields, the objectivity of texts is illusory - e.g. where a semantic distinction is at issue, this information is not actually contained in the text, but has to be imputed to it by the investigator or informant; only in the most exceptional cases does the context of the text allow subtle semantic distinctions to be made without the intervention of a native speaker.

b. by the investigator constructing linguistic data for the approval (or not) of native speakers (who may often be the investigators themselves). This method has the manifest disadvantage of lack of objectivity, when it is compared with looking at texts. However, there is no doubt at all that native speakers give an accurate account of the structures of their language in the vast majority of instances; the problem is that the minority of unclear or inconsistent responses cannot be clearly distinguished except through detailed comparison of different speakers, texts, etc. Intuition is not merely useful, but indispensable, in that texts do not contain negative data - the information that you cannot say such-and-such - nor do they contain many perfectly acceptable structures in sufficient numbers to allow linguists to make generalisations concerning them. Any pretence to be constructing an account of grammar as a whole will therefore be impossible without having recourse to the rich source of data provided by intuitions. And, as mentioned under (a), intuitions are crucial to semantic analysis.

c. by eliciting utterances, judgements, or language-related behaviour in ways which do not involve conscious manipulation of linguistic material by speakers. This would be an ideal compromise between texts and intuitions – it is, in a sense, the creation of texts to order, on the right topic. Unfortunately the method of elicitation confronts severe practical problems, and is more readily suited to certain areas, such as phonology. Labov's famous sociolinguistic research in a department store comes to mind, where he was able to elicit possible environments for postvocalic r by asking where the shoe department was, knowing it was on the fourth floor. But how would you elicit relative clauses or passive sentences using elicitation methods? Obviously it would not do to ask people to produce sentences of a certain form, or give them a model to go on, as you would then be testing their conscious linguistic behaviour, and losing the apparent objectivity of normal linguistic behaviour.

These are effectively the only ways in which we can hope to find the sort of data relevant for linguistic investigation. The most frequently applied procedures in linguistic investigation, and also the most convenient are (a) and (b). (This is by no means a minor matter: the sheer quantity of linguistic data required to reach conclusions in some areas rules out any method where elaborate tests have to be applied to each individual piece of data.) The drawback of (c) is that it requires a very heavy investment of resources of time, money and mental energy for rather minimal returns in reliability of results. (b) is the least reliable of all, but is also the most widely applicable. (a) is more reliable, but not practical for grammatical constructions of low frequency, or where lexical items (other than the few most frequent) are concerned. Moreover, it is impossible to establish that something is ill-formed with (a): contrast the non-occurring but reasonably acceptable sentence of (1) with the non-occurring but quite unacceptable (2):

1. The man who saw it said that the UFO that fired at him was purple
2. The man who John doubted the claim that Mary liked was there

I for one cannot see how there could be a significant syntax without the use of intuitions. At the same time, it is important that careful checks should continually be made, monitoring for possible clues in texts, major disagreements among speakers, and so on.

It is here that, cross-cutting the distinction between text-based and intuition-based data, there is the possibility either of working with what are essentially isolated cases of particular construct- ions or, on the other hand, trying to make some sort of systematic check that one or other type of data is 'typical', or distinguishing areas of variation. At its most basic this simply involves quantity, there being strength in numbers. It becomes relev- ant, for instance, that the passive occurs with a certain frequency, rather than that it simply occurs. More crucially, the linguist can set a threshold of occurrences in a text, or of native speakers giving a particular intuition, below which something will not be recognised as being systemat- ically part of the language. Linguistics books are full of peculiar data, and this applies whether the data happens to have been drawn from a text of some sort (it is still traditional in some circles to take 'good' authors as the standard for linguistic examples, but good authors say some curious things), or from some individual's intuition. Obviously there are possibilities of statistical manipulation here.

Fairly recently there has been much discussion of the possibility of systematic methods for estab- lishing variation between speakers. Such variation might be a function of dialect in the traditional sense - regional variations in language - or it might be a function of social class, or simply of the fact that in some areas of syntax in particular, speakers diverge in what they will say for reasons which are quite obscure, but which nonetheless appear to be systematic. Such studies of variability can be carried out either on intuitions or on texts - there is a natural tendency for psychological studies to concentrate on the former while socio- logical studies concentrate on the latter.

0.3. GENERALISATIONS AND EXPLANATIONS

Any attempt to produce a grammatical account of any area of a language will involve the two closely intertwined concepts of generalisation and explan- ation. We make generalisations by claiming that the solution to one descriptive problem involves essen- tially the same mechanisms as the solution of some other descriptive problem - i.e. by claiming that two separate solutions are in fact one and the same solution, and the phenomena in question are really different facets of the same object. We explain by

giving some reason why things are not other than
they are. The close interrelation between generalisation and explanation relates partly to the fact
that regularity is itself a functionally valuable
property of languages - a language without regularity would be quite unlearnable, and a language with
greater regularity (in some particular area - say
the morphology) than another is _ipso_ _facto_ more
readily learnable. It is also the case that a
higher-order generalisation may itself be generally
accepted as a valid explanation. (Why did I fall
down? Anyone trying to climb up a vertical wall will
fall down.) Any attempt to tease apart what constitutes an explanatory hypothesis and what constitutes a 'mere' generalisation in linguistics is
likely to encounter many problems. I shall therefore
not make this attempt, and on the whole I shall
refer to 'accounting for' the data rather than 'ex-
plaining' it, on the grounds that 'account' can be
used both for things which approach explanatory
status, and for a simple description of events or
facts.

The basic framework that I am referring to is
that of the description of some grammatical phenomenon in a language. Obviously we will be very
gratified if we can produce a simple distributional
statement with respect to a given phenomenon, i.e.
if we can specify that the phenomenon occurs in a
particular set of grammatical environments with a
particular grammatical function. But typically there
will be anomalies of various sorts; our chances of
discovering correlates of these anomalies and providing an account of them in rather general terms
will clearly be enhanced if we have a wider range of
types of correlate against which we can check them.
The following list provides some of the types of
approach which are applicable:

1. Most traditionally, we can start with the
possibility that variation in grammatical phenomena
is likely to be conditioned by purely linguistic
factors - e.g. by phonological criteria, or in syntax or morphology. Considerations of 'euphony' could
be phonological, although such terms should be
viewed with suspicion. Usually, things 'sound wrong'
not because of phonological constraints, but because
they are unacceptable to native speakers, which is
where we came in. Any textbook in linguistics will
provide many examples of variations which are determined by any of these factors, and examples crop up
in most of the chapters of this book.

2. There is some dispute within linguistics

about where the boundary lies between semantics and pragmatics. But the fact that some things are simply 'not the sort of thing you could say' is another obvious fact of relevance to us if we want to establish a basis for restrictions on possible forms. There is no point in developing obscure syntactic devices to perform what is in any case a constraint on subjects of talk, rather than on the form in which they might be expressed. (This is also a pervasive theme of this book, although perhaps not sufficiently so.) Of course this poses problems, in that much indeterminacy is likely to result from introducing such factors. But where the indeterminacy in a phenomenon is introduced because of its nature as a linguistic phenomenon, rather than because of the vagueness of formulation provided by the investigator, then it is hardly possible to criticise this as being inexplicit.

3. Functional factors are a further area of possible explanation; we will, for instance, not be surprised if a language turns out to reject an expressively very powerful mechanism for an area where the expressive power is not needed (cf. chapter 10 on that-complements). Where systematic ambiguity is provoked, we will also find it natural that a language might take steps to avoid it. This of course does not provide us with a theory of the relationship between potential ambiguity and grammatical form - there is a whole literature documenting the problems involved in that area. Conversely, languages may be as complex as they are largely because there are so many types of content which need to be expressed (cf. chapter 3). The important point for the descriptive linguist is that such considerations do provide an intuitively interesting account of certain restrictions, and it is necessary to compile detailed and convincing accounts of such phenomena before we are likely to have any theoretical synthesis.

4. Historical factors also influence the nature of certain constructions. I am not here referring to idiosyncratic historical facts, which may give an account of specific exceptions to a rule - e.g. such and such a verb has a limited range of complementation because it was borrowed within a phraseological unit from Amharic in the sixteenth century, and has remained within that general syntactic frame. However, perhaps particularly in English, there is the contrast between Romance and Germanic elements in vocabulary, and the syntactic and morphological patterns that go along with these elements can be

shown to result in a number of systematic contrasts. Admittedly, the correlation of these phenomena with the historical facts is not perfect, but then it is hardly reasonable to expect English speakers to retain some 'collective memory' of historical development. No doubt any feelings that native speakers now have about such divisions are more in terms of criteria such as 'learned'-'non-learned', or 'posh'-'normal'.

5. Frequency of occurrence is another fact which turns out to be relevant in grammatical analysis. There is a traditional, and intuitively fairly obvious, relationship between frequency and morphological irregularity. The argument goes like this: children learn morphological patterns – essentially a set of regularities – and also a number of irregularities with respect to these patterns. It is reasonable to expect that such irregularities will need to be encountered a number of times before they are learned as such. Low frequency words will not be encountered very often – and certainly not in the range of forms which would be needed to reinforce the irregularity of these words. Therefore they will be assumed to be regular.

6. Anomalies may result from genuine dialect differences, from socio-stylistic factors, or from the sort of unpredictable variability found among speakers (at least we assume it is unpredictable – there is no possible proof). It is unlikely that genuine dialect differences will pose serious problems for long, as they are on the whole found at a fairly high level of consciousness. But the other types are more difficult. In order to discover whether such variation really is affecting the reliability of our data, we need to have recourse to some fairly elaborate and time-consuming techniques. Obviously, therefore, this is not the sort of area to leap into at the beginning – it is when grammatical phenomena appear to defy other types of analysis that these techniques can be wheeled on.

7. It is always possible that phenomena are indeed irregular or idiomatic. We cannot assume this on first coming across data, because it is often very much easier merely to accept idiosyncrasy rather than make the effort to find generalisations. The whole of linguistics is predicated on the assumption that language is **on the whole** regular. Having recourse to irregularity is therefore an admission of defeat – that we have looked in all possible places and failed to find an acceptable solution. Of course such an admission is always

provisional - anyone is entitled to come up with a regular solution if they can find one, and this will clearly be superior to a claim of irregularity, other things being equal.

0.4. REGULARITY AND IRREGULARITY - GRAMMAR AND DICTIONARY

It is quite widely accepted - both among linguists and in general - that the dictionary is the place to put irregular properties of particular words. But how far does irregularity permeate language? Some recent work suggests that, given a large enough number of syntactic properties, no two words behave in grammatically identical ways. It is not difficult to establish apparent irregularity. In fact we shall see a lot of it throughout this book. But are these constructions really irregular? If we took into account the meaning of all of these verbs, would we not be able to say that a large proportion of these apparent irregularities were regular? I believe (as an article of faith) that languages are to a large degree regular. Even if that were not true, such regularity as there is could not be appreciated and established if we did not assume it was there, or if we failed to look for it actively. I shall therefore be looking actively (some might say desperately) for general principles underlying all types of construction. Even where there is manifestly irregularity of some sort, we are faced with the problem of how far partial regularities go, and of what to do with these when we find them. I shall therefore be working for much of the time in just that area which falls between the generalities of the grammar book and the idiosyncrasies of the dictionary.

One of the problems with this type of distinction is that too often it falls prey to the mania for absolute clarity of distinctions among many linguists. Either something should be wholly regular, in which case it is a grammatical phenomenon, or else it is wholly idiosyncratic, in which case it is a lexical phenomenon. Languages are not like that - partial regularity is a fact of linguistic life, and it is one of the features of certain recent approaches to language that this fact is becoming recognised as something which has to be incorporated into anything which can claim to be a theory of language. Here I shall not be concerned, on the whole, with this type of theory; but the essential insight is a crucial one.

It remains true, however, that even given an acceptance that there is a continuous gradation between regularity and irregularity, individual cases cannot a priori be defined as one or the other without examining them in great detail, and attempting to find as many regular aspects of their behaviour as possible. It is important to note that the linguist's division of work into that of grammar and dictionary is a **theoretical** distinction, and does not automatically correspond to the division of labour between actual grammars and dictionaries. Most obviously, particular grammars and dictionaries are likely to be aimed at particular readerships, and it will be possible to omit certain points which a theoretician would wish to see there, and to include others which a theoretician would prefer to see elsewhere. It is a fact of life for those who write **practical** grammars or dictionaries that it is not possible to wait for the resolution of theoretical issues before the work is completed. Nor do average users want to be confronted with the admission that what they are reading is highly contentious, not really justified, or merely inserted as a cover for ignorance. But those of us who are concerned about the description of language in general, or those who use grammars and dictionaries professionally (e.g. language teachers) need to be aware of the status of the information contained in these works. The ability to read standard reference works more critically is something which all of us should aim for; coming to grips with the problems posed by descriptive linguistics and discovering the shortcomings of the existing literature can only serve to increase our respect for the better works of reference.

0.5. A BIBLIOGRAPHICAL NOTE

Each chapter of this book has a bibliographical section at the end. But certain works are relevant to all of the chapters, and it is worth mentioning the major sources of general reference on English. The greatest work of English lexicography is the Oxford English Dictionary (universally known as the OED). The main body of this dictionary was completed in 1927 (it is a continuing enterprise, with three out of four supplementary volumes now published), so it can hardly be said to incorporate the latest advances in linguistic methodology. However, its vast scale, and the care and skill with which it was compiled, make it an indispensable source of reference on English words and their use, both in terms of (relatively) modern usage, and in terms of historical development. The OED is not a work of rapid reference; there are many medium-sized general dictionaries which you will find useful to refer to, and comparison of these various dictionaries is a fascinating pastime in itself, as well as providing useful insights into different ways of approaching descriptive problems. There is also a wide range of more specialised types of dictionaries, some of which will be referred to in later chapters.

Of the major grammars of English the most helpful are the following four: O. Jespersen _A Modern English Grammar_ on _Historical Principles_ (1909-49), London & Copenhagen (seven volumes); E. Kruisinga _A Handbook of Present-Day English_ (1931-2), Groningen; H. Poutsma _A Grammar of Late Modern English_ (1926-9), Groningen; and R. Quirk, S. Greenbaum, G. Leech and J. Svartvik _A Grammar of Contemporary English_ (1972), London. (Henceforth 'GCE' - the others will be referred to by their author's surname.) The latter is the most recent, based on a corpus of English usage, and hence provides the best reflection of contemporary English. The others are based on very extensive sampling of (mainly written) English: they all contain large quantities of fascinating data, not all of it reflecting modern English usage, but invaluable for the student of English. Of these Jespersen is soundest in his judgement, arguably the greatest English grammarian ever. Some of these grammars have spawned baby grammars which are handier to use, and there are numerous other one-volume accounts of English grammar. One other work which will be referred to fairly frequently is F. R. Palmer _The English Verb_ (1975), London - covering many of the same topics covered here, although with very substantial differences of aim and emphasis.

READING - INTRODUCTION

There is a wide literature on problems connected with the data of linguistics. There are many works in 'variation theory'; for an introduction cf. J. K. Chambers and P. Trudgill _Dialectology_, Cambridge 1980, which also contains references to much of the literature. G. Carden _English Quantifiers_ New York: Academic Press 1982, gives an account of one area of variation which does not correlate directly with geographical factors, but appears to characterise speakers of English in a near-random fashion; note, however, that there is a lot of controversy about this work. Labov's elicitation of postvocalic r is reported in W. Labov The Social Stratification of English in New York City, Washington D.C.: Center for Applied Linguistics, 1966 (pp.63-89). G. Sampson The Form of Language, London: Weidenfeld, 1975 suggests that intuitions should not form the primary data of linguistics - but the relevance of his position for actual descriptive practice is obscure. The indeterminacy of many grammatical phenomena is argued cogently by P. Matthews Syntax, Cambridge, 1982.

The notion of a pragmatic account of linguistic phenomena can be approached through the recently published textbook of S. C. Levinson Pragmatics, Cambridge, 1983, which treads very carefully through one of the minefields of linguistics. 'Functional' approaches to language have tended to consist of a ragbag of individual interesting ideas; one of the more systematic attempts at a functional approach, which has a lot of interest to say, is T. Givón On Understanding Grammar, New York: Academic Press, 1979. On the inseparability of grammatical and lexical information, the most substantial study is on French, e.g. M. Gross Méthodes en syntaxe, Paris: Hermann, 1976.

Chapter One

TENSE AND ASPECT

The basic structural form of the English verb group
is quite well known and poses few problems; furthermore, the details have been analysed many times in
the literature (from virtually every theoretical
perspective). We can analyse it as follows, omitting
the specification of which suffixes are appropriate
on the various elements:
    1. (Modal) (have + suf) (be + suf) V + suf
           [Perfect] [Progressive]
This formula begs certain questions: how are the
suffixes specified? does the order of elements in
the verb group need to be specified arbitrarily, or
does it follow from more general principles? what is
the categorial status of all of these elements?
These are questions that have been beaten to death
in the transformational literature, their major
characteristic being that they bear on the types of
grammatical device available in linguistic theory. I
shall not be concerned with these questions, but
rather with the meaning of these various options,
and the problem of their compatibility with different verbs.
    There is a useful distinction to be made
between 'tense' and 'aspect', both of which are
found in English. Tense is a category which primari-
ly involves the time of the event or state specified
by the verb relative to the moment of utterance;
aspect, on the other hand, is notoriously difficult
to define: it is perhaps best to see it as focusing
round such concepts as completion, repetition,
habituality, etc. Look first at the category of
tense in English: any of the positions marked
'suffix' in (1) are in principle available to be
filled with a tense marker (which on the most regular of verbs corresponds to -0,-s or -ed). It is
sometimes assumed that English has three tenses –

past, present and future - but in fact there are
only two relevant formal distinctions in English (-0
and -s are of course a single option, the difference
between them not being a matter of tense, but rather
the person and number of their subject noun phrase).
For instance, with a simple verb, (2) and (3)
exhaust the range of relevant forms:
2. The vicar laughs
3. The vicar laughed
The same distinction is found with the progressive
form (4) and the perfect (5):
4. a. The vicar is laughing
   b. The vicar was laughing
5. a. The vicar has arrived
   b. The vicar had arrived
It is normally (and in accord with general intuition) claimed that these two options represent
present and past tense in English. If we assume that
these labels mean respectively that the action takes
place at the same time as the time of speech, and
that the action precedes the time of speech, then
certain anomalies become apparent:
6. a. Tomorrow we leave
   b. I was walking along, when up comes this
      man, and ....
   c. Do it if you like.
7. a. If you wanted to you could make a lot of
      money
   b. I wish you enjoyed your work more
   c. That animal you saw was probably a mole
None of the underlined verb forms in (6) refers in
any simple way to the time of utterance - as the
adverb in (6a) shows very clearly. Similarly the
verb forms in (7) do not refer to a time preceding
the utterance in any clear way - in (7c), for instance, there is no implication that the animal was a
mole then, but is no longer one. Although I shall on
occasion continue to use labels such as 'past' and
'present', it is as well to recognise that these
labels are far from satisfactory as a representation
of the variety of uses of these verb forms, although
they may be said to reflect what is felt as the most
'typical' uses of these forms.
    A second point to be noted about tense forms
in English is that they behave in rather different
ways when they are describing events which happened
or are expected to happen at some specific time. As
(6a) and (6b) show, the 'present' tense can be used
to refer to events projected into the future, and
also to past events. Naturally enough, the present
tense also refers to present time - the time of

speaking:
    8. I am in a telephone kiosk
But the past tense, when used with specific time
reference, can only refer to events which have
preceded the time of speech (the characteristic of
the sentences in (7) is that they are not used with
reference to any specific time); whereas (8) can be
used in the 'historic present' to narrate events
which happened in the past, (9) cannot be used with
reference to present time or future time:
    9. I was in a telephone kiosk
It is for this reason that many linguists prefer to
talk of English as having a two-way tense distinction between past and 'non-past'. There is one
construction often referred to as a possible exception here - the use of the past tense in a way which
indicates (politely) the present intentions of the
speaker:
    10. I was wondering if you would sign this form
                    for me
Clearly this counts as a request. An alternative way
of treating it would be to say that this use really
is a past tense use - it indicates that the
speaker's intention was in the past, and the interpretation as a request is softened by the fact that
the speaker is no longer claiming to have that
intention. There is always a potential difference
between what the speaker **says** and what the speaker
intends, and this seems to be a case where there is
a fairly clear difference between them.

EXERCISE 1

There is some doubt as to whether the category of
tense is marked in the modal verbs in English. Look
at the following data (and any more you care to
invent), and try to decide what is at issue here:
    11. a. Last year I could beat him at squash but
               now I can't
        b. He can't swim, though he said he could
        c. You could do better than that if you
               tried
        d. Will he come? He wouldn't yesterday
        e. Would you like a drink?
(Remember that the class of modals includes at least
the following forms as well: <u>shall</u>, <u>should</u>, <u>must</u>,
<u>may</u>, <u>might</u>). There is a further complication, in
that a modal verb may be followed by <u>have</u>, with
apparently different effects. Can this be considered
an expression of past tense?

12. a. I must have been able to do it last year
    b. I could have done it last year
    c. I ought to have done it by now

One of the ways in which the analysis of tense forms has often been carried out (both for English and in grammatical sketches of other languages) derives from the work of the philosopher Hans Reichenbach. This work starts by postulating three different time points which are relevant in the interpretation of tense. Take, for instance, a sentence such as (13):

13. John had eaten his dinner

Sentences such as this illustrate very clearly the distinction between the time of utterance (S for speech time), the time at which the event described in the utterance took place (E for event time), and a **reference** time (R) - a time with respect to which the event is located. In (13), for instance, the context (probably preceding discourse) must specify a time in the past (preceding the time of utterance) with reference to which we could talk of the event of John eating his dinner having preceded that point. In Reichenbach's notation, this would be (13'):

13'. E - R - S

(i.e. the event precedes the reference time which precedes the speech time.)

E, R and S are not generally separated from each other in this way: the 'basic' tense forms combine at least two of them at any one point. E.g. the present tense in its normal use shows all three of them at the same point:

14. John is eating his dinner

14'. E,R,S

(i.e. event, speech and reference time coincide.)

The simple past tense, as in (15) obviously has the event preceding the time of utterance: but what of the reference time?

15. John ate his dinner

One relevant observation here is that the simple past tense in English is normally used to refer to something which happens at a particular time, often specified by the discourse. Thus, (15) would be inappropriate if it were not clear at what time the dinner-eating had taken place. It therefore seems likely that the reference time should be coextensive with event time, giving:

15'. E,R - S

(i.e. event and reference time coincide, and precede

speech time.)
It seems to follow that a future tense which corresponds in any way to a past tense, would have the specification
16'. $S - E,R$
(i.e. event and reference time coincide, and follow speech time.)
Indeed, it seems to be true that a natural interpretation of a sentence such as (16) involves there being a specific time in the future at which the event will happen:
16. John will tell you how to get there
There have been numerous developments of Reichenbach's approach to tense, and the question of precisely how any particular combination of E, R and S should be interpreted is one that is open to dispute. Indeed, it is not clear to me that one would **always** wish to recognise a reference time in sentences. Those who adopt such a system generally do recognise a reference time for all types of sentence, but it is conceivable that this is only because of a somewhat misplaced devotion to regularity of analysis. A sentence such as (17) or (18) obviously requires us to recognise a speech time and an event time; but what would a reference time be?
17. Attila the Hun killed a lot of people
18. The earth will come to an end
Note, in fact, that (17) is ambivalent in this respect, although I would not wish to claim that it was actually ambiguous; it could presuppose a context such as
17'. That year was not a good one for the country: Attila the Hun killed a lot of people, and the plague killed off many more
On this interpretation there is a natural reference time (that year). But we could also have it in a different context, e.g.:
17". Attila the Hun killed a lot of people, but modern methods of warfare have been infinitely more destructive
In such a context, the fact of Attila the Hun having killed all of these people is important, but the specific time reference is irrelevant. In spite of such reservations and differences of opinion relating to various aspects of the Reichenbach framework, it is a useful and intuitively satisfying tool in the study of tense systems, and the distinctions which it embodies turn out to be among the most crucial ones in tense theory in general.

1.2. MARKEDNESS AND TENSE

The asymmetry of 'past' and 'present' in English reflects the sort of situation which is often discussed in terms of 'markedness'. In a very basic sense, markedness can be looked on as a purely descriptive concept; alternatively it represents a hypothesis as to how languages organise their grammatical categories. This hypothesis can best be specified in terms of the relationship between form and meaning. On the whole, when languages make use of an opposition as a grammatical category of noun (e.g. number, gender) or verb (e.g. mood, tense) this opposition will be expressed by the presence or absence of an affix. Tense in the English verb, and number in the English noun, are normally marked by the presence or absence of a particular suffix. Markedness (in its guise as a genuine hypothesis) involves the claim that the pole of the opposition which is marked by the absence of a suffix is also semantically less specific. E.g. the form <u>lettuces</u> possesses a suffix which is not found in <u>lettuce</u>: it is also more specific semantically, as it can only refer to a number of distinct objects, while the form <u>lettuce</u> can be used to refer to a single object, or some indeterminate number of objects (<u>lettuce-picking</u>), or some undifferentiated mass of vegetable (<u>Fluffy loves lettuce</u>). Similarly with tense forms, the past tense is 'marked' both morphologically and semantically, as it is almost always expressed with a suffix (excluding such exceptional cases as <u>put</u>), and, as we have seen, it is rather specific in meaning. The present tense, by contrast, may be expressed with the bare stem of the verb, and allows a wider range of meaning.

It is important to note that not all linguists who use the term 'markedness' make use of exactly the same notion. At its vaguest, 'marked' in linguistics is used to refer to something which is slightly unusual. Very frequently the formal and semantic sides are separated (at which point, of course, it ceases to be an empirical hypothesis, as opposed to a descriptive tool). One relevant feature of degrees of markedness which has been noted by Greenberg is that unmarked categories tend to display a greater range of internal variation than more marked categories. For instance, in languages which exhibit gender variation in nouns, such as French, the gender distinctions are likely to be more often expressed in unmarked categories (such as singular) than in marked categories (such as plural). So it is not surprising that the definite article in French marks gender distinctions only in the singular (le - masc. sing., la - fem. sing., les - plural). Similarly with tense forms in English, the (unmarked) present tense exhibits person distinctions (like - likes) but there is no parallel set of distinctions in the (marked) past tense (except with 'be').

Of course markedness is only one of many possible ways of approaching the meaning of grammatical categories. The 'common sense' view of grammatical categories, for instance, sees them as expressing two independent and mutually incompatible meanings (e.g. 'singular' referring to individual objects, and 'plural' referring to sets of objects). The singular-plural distinction would then be said to be an **equipollent** opposition - i.e. both poles of the opposition have a specific positive value, unlike a relation involving markedness, where one pole has a positive value, and the other one has merely a negative value. One of the difficulties of choosing between these two conceptions is that much depends on the way in which the central core of meaning of a grammatical category is defined in the first place. One could well imagine a reanalysis of English 'number' forms as involving, say, notions of 'individualisation' and the like, rather than a simple singular-plural distinction. Fairly clearly, the interpretation of the relationship of the two forms would then be different. Is the same sort of reinterpretation also possible with 'tense'?

There is a whole range of complications associated with questions of this sort, and recent years have seen a number of new approaches to the meaning of grammatical categories which overlap with (or interfere with) the approach involving markedness. One of the most productive of these involves the recognition of pragmatic factors which work on fairly rudimentary semantic properties and elaborate them in accordance with situational and conversational factors. Assume, for instance, that we are talking about the 'present' and 'past' tenses in English and sentences such as those in (7) above are brought up. We might take three possible approaches to these, which seem to run counter to a simple-minded equation of 'past tense' with 'past time reference'. A. We could maintain the claim that 'past tense' refers to a point in time prior to the time of utterance, but restrict this meaning to instances where a specific time reference is understood. In other circumstances, we could claim that it had a quite different meaning, e.g. in conditional sentences or with a verb such as <u>wish</u>, it would have 'unreal' or 'counterfactual' meaning. An approach of this type is commonly used for pedagogical purposes, where use in specific contexts is all-important. While this may be a useful way of presenting data, it fails to treat tense forms as showing any overall unity of meaning, and it will therefore fail to appeal to many linguists.

B. We could decide that (7) justified us in trying to choose a different basic meaning for the 'past tense' - one which would encompass all of the different uses of 'past tense' without actually referring to 'pastness'. This would remain within the confines of a theory of markedness without necessarily invoking pragmatic factors. (Some features of such an approach are sketched in the next section.)

C. A 'pragmatic' approach allows us to give a fairly restricted semantic characterisation of a form, and to account for apparent violations of this characterisation by invoking principles of interpretation which follow from the nature of conversational interaction rather than from purely semantic rules. The historical present in (6b) might be analysed in relation to such an approach; given that it uses the simple form (<u>up comes this man</u>) rather than the progressive it has to be understood as a completed action, and further discourse may well locate it in a string of such actions. It will not be difficult to deduce from context that the type of commentary used in sports reporting is not at issue (that demands both a specific situation and a specific intonation). The characteristically anecdotal content found with the historic present will exclude an interpretation as habitual present (something will hardly be an anecdote worth telling if it is a habitual event). This excludes any of the possible present-time interpretations of such a sentence. If it is being presented as a fact, then it cannot have future reference; this only leaves past time reference as a possibility. By such a tortuous route we can arrive at the fact that it is given a past time interpretation, which is confirmed not only by intuition, but also by the fact that it can co-occur with past tense verbs, past time adverbials, etc.

There are clearly issues behind this sort of approach which need to be confronted, and analyses of other cases which need to be made. The outlines of an overall 'theory of conversational principles' would be needed for a more complete appraisal. But one important consequence is that this 'refinement' plays havoc with the possibility of evaluating specific hypotheses. E.g. if you claim that the distinction we are talking about is a [+/-past] distinction, (7) and (10) appear to be counter-examples. But if they could be dealt with pragmatically, there would be no problems. Only if such proposals were put forward with a semantics and pragmatics fully specified (in the relevant sub-domain) could we evaluate competing possibilities.

I am not claiming that any of these approaches as sketched here represent an adequate account of the problems of tense that we have encountered. Rather, I am claiming that there is a possible development of each of these approaches which in various ways approaches adequacy (although it must be said that there is **no** totally convincing account of even a partial set of tense-related phenomena in English).

1.3. DOES ENGLISH HAVE A CATEGORY OF TENSE?

There is a sense in which this discussion of tense appears quite misleading: in talking of the 'historic present', for instance, we are in fact talking about a use of this form which refers to events which occurred prior to the moment of utterance. Given that 'non-past' is unmarked relative to 'past', we can then claim that it may be used also to refer to past events. But this statement gives only a pale reflection of the ways in which the historic present is actually used, and in particular it fails to capture the fact that the historic present is not used in just **any** context with reference to past events, or to refer to **any** past event or state: cf.
19. A Why don't you go and see your father?
    B *He dies last year
20. *Where are you when I come to see you
        yesterday?
Rather, the historic present appears to occur in contexts where vividness, or immediacy, is desired:
21. I come to see you in the afternoon and where
        are you? Still in bed!
It is to be noted that this type of sentence is extremely colloquial, and it seems that it may vary in line with sociolinguistic factors. It is nevertheless a natural and frequently occurring device of spoken English. We might therefore wish to explore an alternative account of 'present' and 'past' in English. The present is a form specifying 'vivid-

ness' or 'immediacy', and the 'past' is a form specifying 'remoteness' or 'distance'. Three issues seem to arise directly:

i. does English no longer have a tense system?

ii. given markedness, we have a further choice; is this system of forms [+/-vivid], or is it rather [+/-remote]? This has certain consequences if we maintain that the unmarked, negative, form has a wider range of uses.

iii. can we specify this more exactly, and does it have consequences for the 'non-temporal' uses of these forms mentioned in (6) and (7)?

As far as the first issue is concerned, there does not seem to be a great deal of interest to say. If English is analysed as not having a tense system, then it seems likely that the same will be true of many languages. It is not surprising if systems of **aspect** in various languages are analysed as tense systems, because the 'normal' use of a perfective aspect will presumably be to refer to events which have occurred in the past, because events going on at the time of speaking will not be completed: similarly, the 'normal' use of imperfective aspect will be to refer to events currently going on. There is consequently a natural relationship between perfective aspect and past tense, even though it is perfectly possible to envisage specific sentences with different relationships between tense and aspect forms. English, in such a case, would not be very exceptional. The second issue is more interesting: we could in principle claim that all uses of 'present' were 'vivid' and all uses of 'past' were 'remote', and that therefore the issue of markedness did not arise, as the opposition was 'equipollent'. This seems unlikely. Look, for instance, at the contrast between:

22. a. two and two are four
    b. two and two were four

(22a) can hardly be said to be 'vivid', but (b) is decidedly 'remote'; you can see it embedded in contexts such as We all look back with nostalgia to the days when .... If this is typical (and the third issue mentioned above relates to this also), then it would seem that the 'past' is still the marked form, and therefore the tense system would best be characterised on this analysis as [+/-remote].

The third issue is perhaps the most interesting of the three, and can cast further light on the question of markedness. Conditional sentences provide us with perhaps the best examples here:

23. a. If you come, I'll show it to you

b. If you came, I would show it to you

This, as we mentioned above, is obviously not a distinction of time reference: but the feature of remoteness is quite a good characterisation of (b): the possibility of you coming is remote, whereas in (a) it is still a distinct possibility. It is not clear that (a) would be adequately characterised as being 'immediate', or 'vivid' (e.g. the time being envisaged for a visit might be in ten years' time), but non-remote seems fairly appropriate. (It is as well to bear in mind, though, that the plausibility of such judgements **could** be coloured by the fact that English uses <u>remote</u> to refer to possibilities as well as places and times.) Another type of distinction where remoteness also seems more appropriate than tense is the use of sequence-of-tense variations:

24. a. John said he was coming
    b. John said he is coming

Here again, tense is quite inappropriate to distinguish between these two sentences: if you are planning to set off and debating whether to wait for John, both sentences of (24) would indicate that John had expressed his intention to come. The difference is that (b) suggests that the speaker is assuming that John will come, while (a) does not.

There may be other alternative solutions. Leech, for instance, refers to the 'present tense' in English as being 'psychologically present'. Is this any different from saying that it is 'vivid' or 'non-remote'? I find it difficult to say. One of the 'morals' of this discussion seems to be that for any distinction such as the English tense distinction, there are going to be competing hypotheses which **approximately** convey the essence of the distinction. Given notions such as markedness or pragmatic reinterpretation, any of these hypotheses may be shaped to fit in with the apparently exceptional data as well. It therefore becomes an exercise of considerable subtlety to distinguish between the predictions of one such approach and those of another.

EXERCISE 2

Are there ways in which one could test between distinctions such as [+/- past], [+/-remote], [+/-psychologically present], etc.? Are there any further tests which seem to you decisive in favour of one or other of these suggestions? Alternatively,

are there any other distinctions which better convey
the difference between these tense forms?

1.4. THE PRESENT PERFECT AND THE SIMPLE PAST

The grammatical category of **aspect** is to be distinguished from tense, in that tense is most obviously
an expression of time relative to the time of
utterance, whereas aspect expresses the various
phases associated with an action or state (or whatever else is expressed by the verb). It is clear
that the distinction between progressive forms and
simple forms in English (which we shall consider in
the next section) is a distinction of aspect, while
the distinction of present perfect and simple past
is rather more difficult to pin down in terms of
such a distinction. But tradition has it that this
is an aspectual distinction, and there appear to be
no very interesting problems which would result from
quibbling about the terminology.
    The problem with the present perfect is very
simply stated: what is the difference of meaning or
use between (25) and (26)?
    25. John peeled the potatoes
    26. John has peeled the potatoes
Most speakers of English would agree that there is
some difference between these two sentences, yet
pinning down the distinction in terms that are
reasonably precise has turned out to be a very
difficult task. One feature which is shared by
virtually all accounts of the present perfect is the
importance of the notion of 'current relevance'.
According to this idea, the difference between (25)
and (26) is that (25) merely states a fact, as in a
narrative, while (26) presents the same fact as
something which is material to present concerns,
whether these relate to the need to make dinner, or
to something else - e.g. John's usefulness around
the house. In response to a question such as (27),
there is little alternative but to use the simple
past form:
    27. A. What did you do before dinner?
        B. John peeled the potatoes and I jointed
           the chicken
           (*John has peeled the potatoes ...)
By contrast, the present perfect is required where,
for instance, what is at issue is what should be
done now (28) or John's current standing (29):
    28. A. How soon will dinner be ready?
        B. Well, John has peeled the potatoes, so I

should say about 20 minutes.
(cf. *John peeled the potatoes)
29. A. I hope John's not being a nuisance
    B. Not at all: he's peeled the potatoes,
       vacuumed the floors, washed the dishes ...
There are a number of specific cases which are
usually subsumed under the current relevance criterion: one of the classic cases, which also illustrates the rather fluid nature of 'current relevance', has been termed the 'hot news' use of the
present perfect:
    30. The Second World War has ended
Used immediately after the end of the war, (30)
would have been appropriate (assuming the hearer(s)
did not already know this fact). Used to one of the
Japanese soldiers occasionally reported as still
holding out in various remote parts of the Pacific,
it would also be appropriate (if only they understood English!). It could also be natural as a
mildly ironic response to someone expressing great
hostility towards the Germans or the Japanese. In
normal cirumstances, however, it would not be appropriate now (1984). Another aspect of current relevance is the possibility that the message can still
be acted on: one well-known example:
    31. a. Have you seen the Monet exhibition?
        b. Did you see the Monet exhibition?
(31a) suggests that the exhibition is still available to be seen, and that the hearer is in a state
to see it, while (31b) suggests that it is over, or
that the hearer is in a situation which makes it
impossible for him to see it. (31a) might involve
current relevance because, in the event of a
negative answer, the speaker can recommend him to go
(or not) - something which is obviously impossible
if the exhibition is no longer on.
    One of the difficulties with anything as vague
as 'current relevance' is the possibility of its
being applied in such as way as to render it virtually meaningless. One of the uses of the present
perfect is to refer to some, possibly unique, event
in the past; in this use, the auxiliary <u>have</u> is
often stressed:
    32. a. I **have** flown, but I was sick, so I never
           tried it again
        b. I **have** read that book, but it was a long
           time ago
Obviously in cases such as these, one could try to
extend the notion of current relevance by saying
that the present state of the subject is different
from what it would have been had that event not

taken place. However, that could be said about any event in which a person or thing has participated; the suggestion that this is a distinctive character- istic of the present perfect seems quite unreason- able. It is with such examples as these, perhaps, that the major competing (or complementary?) account of the present perfect becomes most compelling - its treatment as an 'indefinite past' tense. As noted above, the simple past tense in English typically has reference to a specific time: if no specific time reference is intended, the simple past is no longer appropriate, and the present perfect is available for use instead.

Again as in section 2 of this chapter it is possible to see that there might be a pragmatic reason why the notion of 'indefinite past' is inter- pretable in some contexts as involving 'current relevance'. A simple past - a 'definite past' - will normally be used to inform someone of what went on at a particular time. An indefinite past obviously cannot be used for this function, and it would therefore be natural to seek some other point for an utterance in the indefinite past. An obvious choice would be to interpret such an utterance as saying something about an event or state with reference to something other than its place in a narrative sequence, given that utterances are typically under- stood as being relevant in some way to some other issue which is currently of importance. Hence current relevance. This process of inference would not provide the present perfect with a specific current relevance interpretation, but then that is what we should want, as the present perfect is not constrained to refer to any one aspect of current relevance. Take (33), for instance:

33. John has had his breakfast

This sentence could be understood as relevant in a variety of ways - that John needs no further feed- ing, as an explanation for the crumbs on the table, to clarify what time it might be, etc. Such reason- ing, then, might suggest that the notion of 'indef- inite past' is both compatible with the notion of 'current relevance' and logically prior to it. The qualifications of section 2 are still relevant here, however: given the richness of devices available to us, it seems unlikely that a clear test can be worked out to decide between such differing hypo- theses.

The applicability of the present perfect is dependent in various ways on the semantics of the verbs which occur in it. One fairly common class of

verbs, for instance, refers to the transition
between one state and another - e.g. vanish, break,
kill, move, etc. The present perfect with these
verbs indicates that the resultant state still holds
true - e.g. (34) would be inappropriate if the
magician had already reappeared:
34. The magician has vanished
With any verb which denotes an instantaneous action
without any necessary result (e.g. hit, pull,
glance, etc.) the 'hot news' interpretation will be
natural, with the speaker waiting to see what will
happen next:
35. John has hit Bill
Where, on the other hand, the verb denotes a state,
with no implied action or event, the present perfect
on its own is rather anomalous; the addition of a
clause beginning with since can rectify this:
36.a.　*John has known the answer to that
　　　　question (unstressed auxiliary)
　　b. John has known the answer to that since
　　　　he was at school
Often a verb of state can occur either with since or
with stressed have, but not otherwise:
37. a.　*John has wondered whether he's right
　　　　(unstressed auxiliary)
　　b. John has wondered whether he's right ever
　　　　since we had that argument
　　c. John **has** wondered whether he's right, but
　　　　usually he suppresses such doubts
From the perspective of the occurrence of the
present perfect with verbs and verb phrases of
various types, there appear to be three distinct
types of construction: when the sentence contains a
temporal since phrase, virtually any verb can occur
with the present perfect, in one interpretation or
another:
38. a.　John has weighed 17 stone since he was
　　　　sixteen
　　b. I have walked to work since I lost my
　　　　licence
　　c. I have known him since we were kids
The construction with stressed have occurs with most
verbs, but not with those which are not used with
reference to changeable states:
39. a.　He **has** weighed 17 stone, but that was
　　　　when he was in a wheelchair
　　b. I **have** walked to work, but it wasn't very
　　　　nice
　　c. *I **have** known him, but not for long
The basic use of the present perfect, with unstressed have, is unlikely to occur with verbs

denoting states:
    40. a. *He's weighed 17 stone
       b. I've walked to work, but I'll get the bus
              back
       c. *I've known him

All of these uses of the present perfect share some of the features of the perfect in general - e.g. they do not occur with temporal adverbs referring to some past time not including the present.

    41. a. *I **have** walked to work in 1975 (said in
              1984)
       b. *I've walked to work in 1975/yesterday

One final point: note that the present perfect is clearly morphologically marked with reference to the simple past. In addition to the simple verb stem, it includes an auxiliary verb which does not characterise the simple past. It also seems reasonably intuitive to claim that the present perfect is semantically marked by comparison with the simple past: the latter is a simple narrative description of the fact that something took place in the past, while the present perfect can be seen as having in addition whatever feature corresponds to 'current relevance'. It may be that this is giving disproportionate emphasis to the notion of narrative; perhaps we should await a comprehensive theory of tense and aspect before committing ourselves.

EXERCISE 3

Collect examples of the present perfect from speech or from your reading. Can you find any which do not conform to the pattern presented here? (and if so, do you find them natural English?) Can you see any ways of tightening up the notion of 'current relevance', or replacing it with a more adequate characterisation of the present perfect?

EXERCISE 4

The text which follows is an extract from a BBC news bulletin: simple past, present perfect and present tenses are used there in apparently similar ways. Examine these uses and try to determine why the tenses are used as they are.

    At the start of the week in which the Conservatives hold their annual conference, there's been further criticism of the Government's

policies from within the party. The former
leader of the House of Commons Mr. Norman St.
John-Stevas, who was dismissed by Mrs. Thatcher
in a Cabinet reshuffle, has called for greater
flexibility. Speaking on 'The World This
Weekend' on Radio Four, he said there was wide-
spread disquiet at what was happening. It could
not be contained by Mrs. Thatcher repeating that
there was no alternative policy. ... But the
Chancellor of the Exchequer Sir Geoffrey Howe
insists that the Government is set on the
correct course. Appearing on the ITV programme
'Weekend World', he said the policies followed
so far were moving the country in the right
direction.

EXERCISE 5

There are presumably limitations to the treatment of
the present perfect as an indefinite past. Explore
the relationship between an indefinite past reading
of the present perfect, and other past forms such as
used to, would, etc.

1.5. THE PROGRESSIVE AND THE SIMPLE FORM

The problem that faces us with the progressive
relates to contrasts such as those of (42):
    42. a. John smiled
       b. John was smiling
The progressive form in (42b) manifestly differs in
function from the simple form in (42a); in any given
context, few speakers of English would have any
difficulty about showing which of these forms was
more appropriate, and what the difference of meaning
was, if any. However, it has proved remarkably
difficult to formulate a satisfactory general
account of the difference between these forms. We
shall illustrate this difficulty with a passage from
Palmer's The English Verb - not because it is
exceptional, but rather because it is part of a
reasonably careful account of temporal and aspectual
phenomena within the English verbal system:

    The progressive indicates activity continuing
    through a period of time - activity with dura-
    tion. The non-progressive merely reports activ-
    ity, without indicating that it has duration.
    This is shown by comparison of:

He walked to the station
He was walking to the station
The first sentence simply gives the information that he walked to the station; the second
indicates that the walking had duration. There
is, of course, no suggestion that there are two
kinds of activity one without and one with duration, but simply that attention is drawn in the
one case to its durational aspect. (Palmer p35)

Before you go on, read the passage from Palmer
very carefully. What is he trying to say? What
predictions can we make, given this passage, about
the likely uses of the simple and the progressive
forms?
It is not at all clear (to me at least) what
Palmer means in this passage. For instance, there
are many verbs which refer to 'instantaneous'
actions, but none of these are incompatible with the
progressive:
43. a. He's reaching the top now
    b. The rock is starting to move
What would it mean for such uses of the progressive
to indicate duration? Note that these verbs do not
allow adverbs of duration:
44. a. *He reached the top for several hours
    b. *The rock started to move for at least
            ten seconds
We also get some odd effects if we put duration
adverbs with other types of verbs too:
45. a. Last night he slept for ten hours
    b. Last night he was sleeping for ten hours
(45a) is a simple report (to use Palmer's terminology) of the duration of his sleeping. (45b) is
decidedly odd if you try to give it this same interpretation. Possibly the most natural interpretation
of (45b) that I can find is the 'intention' use of
the progressive, as in:
46. For the next week I'm keeping off the booze
i.e. (45b) indicates his programme of sleep for the
night, whether or not he achieved it. If you take
away last night, it can be interpreted in an
iterative sense - i.e. as involving repetition of
the action:
47. All of last month he was sleeping for ten
            hours (a night)
Palmer is also forced to conclude (p68) that the
progressive can be used for **limited** duration, as
opposed to the simple form:
48. a. He lives in London
    b. He's living in London

Here the simple form imposes no boundaries on the duration of his residence in London, while the progressive at least suggests that this residence is temporary. In fact this is no more than a suggestion, as it can be used otherwise:

49. He's still living in the same house he's lived in all his life

Possibly the weightiest objection against Palmer's notion that the progressive expresses duration is that it simply focuses on the wrong feature of the progressive - there are instances of the use of the progressive where it quite obviously differs from the simple form, but where talk of 'duration' is completely unsatisfying. Of course it is difficult to say that the progressive does not express duration in most cases - the difference between duration which is expressed in morphological form and duration which we understand because the action expressed by the verb takes time is unlikely to be immediately evident to someone looking at pairs of sentences. But if there is a **different** distinction which seems better able to capture the divergent uses of these forms, we shall obviously prefer it. Consider in this context a pair such as:

50. a. Yesterday he read a book
    b. Yesterday he was reading a book

Talk of duration is simply unhelpful here. As with walking to the station, the duration analysis predicts that the progressive form means the same as the simple form but for the **added** meaning of duration. But in fact the progressive seems to lack one semantic property of the simple form - that of **completion**. (50a) tells us that he read a complete book, while (50b) does not tell us that, but only that at some point yesterday he was reading some portion of the book. In fact, if we assume Grice's Maxim of Quantity (part of which goes 'Be informative') we can be fairly sure that the speaker of (50b) has no evidence that he has finished the book.

How does the notion of completeness square with the rest of the data on progressives that we have looked at so far? With instantaneous actions (43), although they remain slightly peculiar in the sense that an instantaneous but incomplete action seems rather anomalous, incompleteness seems to fit in reasonably well. We would not use (43a) for someone who really had reached the top, but rather for someone on the very last stage towards reaching it; failure is still possible. Similarly, (43b) might reasonably be used if the only visible signs of movement are a few shudders, perhaps with audible signs of movement, but not while the rock is crashing down. Note that there is a different interpretation of 'incompleteness' which becomes possible,for instance, if a different time adverbial is used – i.e. iteration, or repetition, of the event. If we say He's reaching the top quite often these days, it refers to an instantaneous action which is repeated with some frequency, and which the speaker considers will be repeated again in the future. Incompleteness also accounts for the oddity of (45b): the 'for ten hours' puts a natural limit on his sleeping which is not compatible with the notion of incompleteness.

All theories have problems: (48) provides problems for this one. Living is not the sort of thing which naturally fits into a dichotomy of complete and incomplete. Similarly with verbs such as know, be (tall), resemble, etc. It is therefore surely significant that it is precisely verbs of this sort (often called 'stative verbs') which do not typically occur with the progressive. The simple form of the verb, often of very restricted use with verbs of action, is used as the basic form with these verbs (and sometimes the only form):

51. a. John thinks that he is correct
    b. ??John is thinking that he is correct
    c. Mary resembles her mother
    d. *Mary is resembling her mother
    e. Mary is resembling her mother more and
        more these days

(51e) illustrates a rather common use of adverbs such as more and more with the progressive, indicating a continuing (i.e. incomplete) progression towards the state or habit referred to by the verb phrase.

This type of stative verb behaviour illustrates a further point about markedness: when a semantic distinction is **neutralised** – i.e. is inapplicable to elements of a particular type – it is usually the morphologically unmarked form which is used to express the semantically undifferentiated result. I.e. the progressive will tend to be used only in cases where it has a potential semantic contrast with the simple form, but the simple form will also be used where no contrast is possible. With a form like (48b), then, what seems to happen is that there is a further distinction which it seems useful to make. As the progressive is 'unoccupied' in that particular context, it makes sense to use the progressive form to express this further semantic distinction, especially as there does appear to be **some** relationship between the meaning of lack of completion and the meaning of temporariness. If this suggestion is accepted, it constitutes a further reason why it may be exceedingly difficult to choose between competing accounts of the same phenomena: 'loose ends' such as these cannot be reliably distinguished from more 'central' uses of the progressive.

EXERCISE 6

Taking a basic sentence such as
        John is fiddling his tax
describe the changes in interpretation which happen when the present perfect auxiliary <u>have</u> is added, and when one or more of the following modifiers is added, in the appropriate position:
        not, these days, always, for the last two years
How do these various usages fit in with the general picture of the progressive painted above?

EXERCISE 7

Listen to some sports reporting (preferably of a fast-moving sport like football, rugby, tennis, etc.); how are the progressive and the simple present used? Are they used in a way which is compatible with anyone's theory of the difference between these forms?

READING - CHAPTER 1

B. Comrie <u>Aspect</u>, Cambridge, 1976, is a careful general study, bringing in tense as well, insofar as the two notions interact. It is not restricted to English, but has much to say about many languages. J. Lyons <u>Semantics</u>, Cambridge, 1977, also has much of interest to say about tense and aspect, especially in its second volume (chapters 15 and 17). The position of tense and aspect markers in the English auxiliary system has been a recurring theme of transformational grammar; compare the two quite different positions of N. Chomsky <u>Syntactic Structures</u>, The Hague: Mouton, 1957, and G. K. Pullum and D. Wilson 'Autonomous syntax and the analysis of auxiliaries', <u>Language</u>, 53, 741-88, 1977. There has been a mushrooming of recent studies on the semantics of tense and aspect, and some of these are represented in volume 14 of the series

Syntax and Semantics - Tense and Aspect, New York: Academic Press, 1981; some of the papers in this volume are quite difficult to read, it should be noted. Some are based on the work of Hans Reichenbach on tense - an appendix to his Elements of Symbolic Logic, London: Macmillan, 1947. Pragmatic approaches, although not specifically in detail on tense, are interestingly presented in S. Levinson Pragmatics, Cambridge 1983, which also deals with Gricean principles. On the 'historic present' see N. Wolfson 'The conversational historical present alternation', Language 55, 168-82, 1979.

For markedness, the earliest work was done in the Prague school tradition, notably, in relation to grammatical categories, by Roman Jakobson; several articles in this framework appear in his Selected Writings, vol. 2, The Hague: Mouton, 1971. J. Greenberg Language Universals, The Hague: Mouton, 1966 gives a good general account of the notion, with much relevant data. It should be noted that a recent use of the word 'markedness' in 'Government and Binding' theory is largely distinct from the traditional notion, although related in some rather vague sense. An interesting attempt to link markedness and frequency is P. H. Tiersma 'Local and general markedness' Language, 58: 832-49, 1982.

Specifically on aspect, there is a useful discussion in W. H. Hirtle The Simple and Progressive Forms: an Analytical Approach, Quebec: Presses de l'Universite Laval, 1967, and in J. Scheffer The Progressive in English Amsterdam: North Holland, 1975. There is now a great deal of work in this area in the formal semantics literature, which, it must be said, tends to be of great complexity and is not to be attempted lightly. One useful work which is more readable than its title suggests is D. Dowty Word Meaning and Montague Grammar, Dordrecht: Reidel, 1979. The articles in the Syntax and Semantics volume mentioned above will also be useful.

Chapter Two

TRANSITIVITY

The categorisation of verbs as transitive and
intransitive is often felt to be a major part of the
description of their syntactic behaviour. Most
dictionaries, for example, will provide the information that a verb is transitive or intransitive, or
both, but will not systematically provide any other
syntactic information. We can exemplify this dist-
inction with verbs such as <u>wield</u>, <u>contain</u>, <u>dislike</u>,
etc. (transitive) and <u>emerge</u>, <u>vanish</u>, <u>elapse</u>, etc.
(intransitive), each of which is fairly close to the
behaviour of their 'ideal' type, as <u>wield</u> is almost
totally restricted to occurring with a following
noun phrase, while <u>emerge</u> cannot be followed by an
object noun phrase. These ideal types, however, are
not entirely typical in English, most verbs allowing
a rather greater range of contexts of occurrence. It
is here that the limitations of a categorisation
into transitive and intransitive become apparent;
there are many different ways in which the transitive and intransitive uses of a verb can correspond
to each other. This is one area where the demarc-
ation between dictionaries and grammars becomes
troublesome; should we try to produce some more
refined classification of transitivity properties so
that it can be used in dictionaries? Or should we
perhaps attempt to give each different type of
transitive or intransitive use of verbs some general
characterisation, so that their grammatical
behaviour should follow from, say, their meaning?
Some idea of the range of grammatical behaviour
in this area needs to be given. Without claiming to
give an exhaustive list, we can distinguish the
following classes of verbs (some justification for
the more contentious distinctions will be given
later):
(i) so-called 'ergative' verbs (a term borrowed

from a rather exotic grammatical construction which occurs in many of the languages of the world), which occur both transitively and intransitively, the subject of the intransitive being the same as the object of the transitive, e.g. verbs like disperse, melt, roll, break, open, turn, etc.

    1. a. John opened the door
       b. The door opened

Some grammarians distinguish within this class a set of verbs (such as walk, gallop, run, etc.) where the intransitive verb involves volitional activity, cf.:

    2. a. The soldiers marched over the cliff
       b. The general marched his soldiers over the
          cliff

    (ii) 'pseudo-intransitive' or 'derived intransitive' verbs are rather like ergative verbs, but their intransitive uses are rather more restricted by comparison - e.g. polish, wash, sell, read, etc. (cf. section 4 of this chapter for details.)

    3. a. I read Chomsky's new book
       b. Chomsky's new book reads like a thriller

    (iii) 'object-deleting' verbs, which occur both transitively and intransitively while retaining the same subject- e.g. read, write, eat, cook, swallow, etc.

    4. a. An old lady swallowed a fly
       b. The old lady swallowed hard

    (iv) verbs (for which there is no accepted name) where the transitive object is changed in some way (usually specified in a prepositional phrase) by the (intransitive) action performed by the subject:

    5. a. His boss shouted (at Bill)
       b. His boss shouted Bill out of the door
    6. a. The salesman talked (to Bill)
       b. The salesman talked Bill into buying a car

    (v) there is also a substantial number of modifications which appear relatively idiosyncratic to individual verbs or constructions, but which affect the apparent transitivity of sentences:

    7. a. The poor man squirmed
       b. The poor man squirmed his way out of the
          room
    8. a. He laughed
       b. He laughed a very dirty laugh

(8) represents the construction with 'cognate objects' - either morphologically identical, or semantically very similar, to the verb.

    (vi) and (vii) finally there are verbs which may only be used intransitively or transitively respectively - the 'pure' transitives or intransitives. There are comparatively few of these among the more frequent English verbs.

Numerous questions arise about a typology such as this. It appears that some of these categories are a matter of degree rather than simple yes/no features. All of the verbs that are mentioned under (iii), for instance, can be said to have quite normal intransitive uses; you can swallow without swallowing anything, and sentence (9) does not imply any specific object:

9. Little Willie is writing/reading/eating very well these days

But there are many other verbs which can be used intransitively only in much more restricted circumstances:

10. Will you pour?
11. We have a very efficient arrangement with our logs; he chops and I pile

A sentence such as (10) is only appropriate in a very limited stereotype situation (tea drinking), while in (11), the objects of <u>chop</u> and <u>pile</u> are specified in the immediate context. In other circumstances they would be significantly less acceptable. Similar uncertainties arise for most of the other classes as well. Nor is it sufficient simply to say that (10) and (11) involve ellipsis: these cases, as well as being highly marginal with respect to any attempt at a clear delimitation of transitivity, are also highly marginal with respect to ellipsis. When is it reasonable to say that a verb is being used intransitively, as opposed to the same verb used with ellipsis of the direct object? There is a wide range of opinions and definitions in this area, and I make no claim to definitiveness. However, it is perhaps possible to bring in contexts in which the distinction between genuine intransitive uses of otherwise transitive verbs, and semi-elliptical uses will be made fairly clearly:

12. I'm inventing a machine: it will be able to
    (a) write
    (b) write novels
    (c) *chop
    (d) chop wood

(12b) and (12d) give fairly straightforward characterisations of what the machine can do. (12a) can be interpreted in at least two different ways; either the machine is able to manipulate the elements of narration and produce stories, perhaps, or else it can manipulate a writing instrument and produce something that looks more or less like handwriting. The first of these interpretations might conceivably be interpreted as involving ellipsis of a noun like

stories; the second interpretation cannot be interpreted in this way - i.e. it is a genuinely intransitive use of the verb write. (12c) cannot be interpreted in this intransitive way; we could imagine a
machine which took a cutting instrument like an axe,
and systematically moved it up and down. You would
not say of such a machine That machine can chop; you
might be tempted to say that it can indeed produce
chopping actions, but would it actually chop wood if
there was some wood in the way of its axe, or would
the action perhaps not be forceful enough to make an
impression on the wood? The same action might
successfully chop (ice cream, for instance) and fail
to chop (wood). In other words, write carries within
itself a notion of result, while chop can only be
interpreted as having a result given a particular
thing which is chopped.

2.2. THE NOTION 'DIRECT OBJECT'

Part of the difficulty with constructions of this
type is that the notion of transitivity is normally
defined in terms of the notion 'direct object' (DO),
which in turn is not at all transparent in its
usage, even though it plays a part in much current
linguistic theory. The following are a number of the
criteria for DO-hood which have been proposed in the
literature on English:
     (i) a DO is a noun phrase which immediately
follows a verb
     (ii) a DO is a noun phrase which can be made
into a subject by the passivisation rule. (I assume
you know what a subject is; for passives, see the
next three chapters.)
     (iii) a DO is a noun phrase whose referent is
affected by, or created by, the action of the verb.
     (iv) a DO is one of the noun phrases which a
verb is **required** to occur with (i.e. it is **selected**
by the verb). (This criterion does not distinguish
DOs from subjects or indirect objects, but it does
distinguish them from many other types of noun
phrase.)
     No doubt this is not an exhaustive list, but it
certainly includes most of the criteria which are
current. Of course, if we wanted to distinguish
objects from subjects, there would be a whole host
of criteria that we could call upon; but naturally
enough this is not a question which is tremendously
troublesome for English. What we need is something
which will distinguish DOs from other things which

follow the verb in English sentences.

EXERCISE 1

Look at sentences (1)-(8) above, and also at the sentences of (13) below. Which of them involve DOs by any of the criteria mentioned here? Which of them do **you** think are DOs? Do your intuitions coincide with any of the criteria, or with any combination of the criteria? If not, can you think of some other criterion (or criteria) which might work?
    13. a. They danced all night
        b. They went that way
        c. Who did you see?
        d. John resembles Mary
        e. He weighs a ton
        f. John is a lion-tamer
        g. John gave Mary a book
        h. Elephants trampled over my cabbage patch
        i. Out went the light
        j. John likes Mary
        k. He emerged the victor

    There are at least two distinct approaches that we can take if we find that a familiar concept is virtually impossible to pin down adequately with the criteria to hand. Either we attempt to refine our criteria and add to them in such a way that the notion we recognise intuitively corresponds more closely to what is defined by our criteria, or else we stop and ask ourselves: why do we need this concept? Are we perhaps trying to fit a number of incompatible phenomena into a pigeonhole which happens to be there? Obviously it would be nice to know which noun phrases could be promoted to subject in passive constructions; we shall consider just this question in chapter 4. Similarly we would be very satisfied if we came across a nice explanation of why some verbs fit into the ergative pattern, others into the 'object-deleting' pattern, etc. But it is not at all clear that the same notion of 'direct object' needs to be specified independently of the particular construction that we are investigating.
    What we shall do in the rest of this chapter, therefore, is to look at the verb classes mentioned at the beginning of this chapter, to see if they are predictable from any semantic or syntactic factors. Of course, it could be that the question of which

verbs fit into which classes is purely a matter of historical accident, and needs to be specified lexically, for each verb. However, if we do not assume the likelihood of regularity, we are unlikely to find any; there is never any problem in finding apparent anarchy. I shall allow myself to be fairly crude in terms of the sources of data which I make use of, as, although the data being discussed are often problematic, there does not seem (so far as I can judge from informal observation) to be enormous variation in judgements across speakers - i.e. relative acceptability is on the whole constant across speakers.

2.3. OBJECT-DELETION AND ERGATIVITY

Object-deleting and ergative verbs share the general property that they both have transitive and intransitive uses, and also that their use is heavily dependent on the lexical properties of the verbs themselves, rather than on contextual factors or on other aspects of the structure of the sentence. We can therefore list verbs which do and do not occur in these constructions in a way which would hardly be possible with, say, 'pseudo-intransitives'. Tables 1 and 2 do precisely this. Obviously we can choose to list as extensively as we wish - these lists are rather short; but the point of any such exercise has to be to look at the classes of verbs involved from the point of view of saying why it is that they have different syntactic properties. Looking at the tables, the following observations emerge with some clarity:
   A. The ergative verbs are without exception verbs of change of physical or mental state or location. Only a smallish proportion of the object-deleting verbs (cut, clean and build are all clear cases) are of this semantic class. If you cook something, for instance, it changes to a cooked state, whereas if you accept, answer or forget something, that thing is not automatically changed thereby.
   B. In Table 2, change, move, turn, walk and work are all in the 1000 most frequent words in English. None of the other list is in that class, and therefore we might suggest that ergative behaviour is contingent on 'familiarity' as well as on semantic factors.
   C. If we contrast a verb such as cut with one like break, we can see that cut is associated both

Table 2.1   Some verbs of different classes

Object-deleting verbs	Ergatives	Neither
accept	break	admit
add	burn	allow
answer	change	attempt
ask	close	bear
bite	cook	beat
blow	drop	believe
build		bring
buy?		carry
call		catch
clean		clear
consider		command
cook		complete
count		contain
cross		control
cut		cover
direct		demand
draw		destroy
drink		discover
drive		enjoy
eat		expect
enter		express
explain		favour
fight		fill
follow		find
forget		force
gain		gather

Table 1 is extracted from a list of those verbs which are among the 1000 most frequent words in English. This list is not representative of all meanings of these verbs - e.g. <u>believe</u> can be used intransitively in a religious sense, but not in the sense of <u>I believe you</u>, for instance, which I take to be its most frequent type of use. Of course you may disagree with some of these judgements, and I may have overlooked some quite plausible uses.

with a characteristic action (a blade-like thing being drawn vertically across a surface) and with a characteristic result (a clean separation between two surfaces), while <u>break</u> is associated only with a characteristic result, and not at all with an action. Whatever one does with the result that the

Table 2.2. Some related verbs differing in behaviour

Ergative	Non-ergative
change	transform
move	transfer
topple	upset
turn	convert
twist	writhe
vary	differ
vibrate	throb
walk	wander
work	toil
worry	trouble

Table 2 is a rather more random assemblage of words which can be used ergatively (strictly speaking, some of them fit in a 'causative' class) coupled with words which mean rather similar things, but which cannot be used ergatively.

window shatters, we will talk about having broken the window, but if you give a karate chop to a piece of wood and it splits cleanly in two by virtue of some quirk of the grain, we will not say that you cut it. This is a rather indeterminate distinction, and also one which is rather clearer on verbs which refer to physical action than on other verbs; however, object-deleting verbs tend to be more like cut, where the action depends, at least to some extent, on what the subject does, while the other classes tend to be more like break, where the action is so called because of what the object does, albeit under the direct influence of the agent. If this is true it is fairly natural: if the object is so crucial it is not surprising that it cannot be omitted. For similar reasons, verbs like cut and build are not ergative: although they express a change of physical state, they also express a characteristic action performed by some agent, while ergative verbs do not presuppose any agent at all.

These observations are all relevant to the syntactic behaviour of verbs, but more extensive scrutiny reveals certain problems: e.g. why are sentences such as those of (14) not possible?

14. a. *John killed yesterday (= 'died')

       b. *Over the years the building has cleaned
          considerably
       c. *That remark made yesterday
Their unacceptability suggests that there must be
more to the characterisation of ergative verbs than
I have done so far. (Here as always, of course,
there is the other alternative that these properties
merely constitute historical accidents; however, the
approach that I am taking is to **assume** a degree of
regularity, and therefore I shall not consider this
possibility.)

EXERCISE 2

Improve on the analysis of object-deleting verbs and
ergative verbs as given above. This might involve
some of the following steps:
    - examine the explicitness of my criteria and
test it by trying to divide up the verbs in Tables 1
and 2 by the criteria rather than their behaviour.
    - suggest more examples which pose difficulties,
either in being ill-defined by the criteria as
stated, or else in being straightforward counterexamples to my claims.
    - propose refinements of these criteria, or
completely new criteria, which you think might
either better account for my data with your additions, or serve as further conditions for the acceptability of these constructions.

2.4. ERGATIVES AND PSEUDO-INTRANSITIVES

Ergative and pseudo-intransitive (PI) sentence
patterns are clearly similar in some respects, with
the object of the transitive verb showing the same
range of restrictions as the subject of the intransitive form. The similarity goes rather further; for
every intransitive use of an ergative verb, there
appears to be another use which is indistinguishable
from a PI sentence:
    15. Suddenly the window broke (Ergative)
    16. Be careful, that window breaks easily (PI?)
There are three major criteria by which we can
distinguish ergative and PI sentences. Firstly there
is the semantic criterion that a sentence such as
(15) refers to a specific event, while a PI sentence
like (16) is **generic** in the sense that it refers to
the propensity of the window to break, rather than
to any specific event that has happened, or which is

projected. The second criterion, also a semantic one, is that PI sentences do not make sense unless the possible activity of an agent is envisaged, while the intransitive use of ergative verbs involves no suggestion that an agent is at work. (15) reports that the window broke, but it makes no reference to what may have caused the breakage. By contrast, (16) is not compatible with an interpretation that the window is liable to break spontaneously - only that the external force required to break it is not substantial. The third difference between these uses is that the PI sentence typically involves some adverbial determination of the verb; typical examples of this are <u>easily</u>, <u>well</u>, negation, and phrases beginning with <u>like</u>:

    17. a. This material washes well
       b. The door won't shut
       c. American cars handle like oil tankers

A supplementary criterion can be established by the use of coordination, which tends to apply to elements of a similar sort; some verbs are usable in PI sentences but not in an ergative construction, and when ergative verbs are coordinated with these, it is fairly clear that the whole construction has to be interpreted as PI:

    18. a. This cup won't scratch or break
       b. *This cup scratched and broke

However, it must be said that the boundaries between ergative and PI uses are far from clear, and it is not always possible to tell whether a given sentence is one or the other - cf. the following example from a psychology journal:

    19. The magnitude of the California effect has failed to replicate on at least a couple of occasions.

In this connection it is also worth noting a now-archaic use of the progressive as a voice-neutral form, which was still quite common in nineteenth-century English; Jespersen brings the following examples, from Scott and Austen respectively:

    20. a. while these measures were taking ...
       b. while the parcels were bringing down and displaying on the table...

It is a fairly commonplace observation that pseudo-intransitive sentences can be formed from action verbs only. In other words, we do not have sentences such as (21), even though it would not be difficult to interpret them as indicating some general characteristic of the subject:

    21. a. *Mary dislikes all too easily

      b. *Subversive thoughts don't think in such
          circumstances
      c. *Such situations imagine easily

But it is not the case that all action verbs allow the formation of PI sentences:

    22. a. *My savings won't withdraw
        b. *These rock buns eat quite easily
        c. *French learns more easily than Russian

In fact there are 'minimal pairs' of quite similar meaning which differ in terms of their ability to form PI sentences:

    23. a. His books sell like hot cakes
        b. *His books buy like hot cakes
    24. a. John shocks rather easily
        b. *John distresses rather easily
    25. a. Laing's articles read like parodies
        b. *That programme watched like a
          documentary
    26. a. This carpet beats clean
        b. *John beats quite easily (at tennis)

One possible line of approach to data such as this is the following: when we try to form sentences on the PI pattern, we are saying that it is a characteristic of the subject that it undergoes the action of the verb with a certain result, or in a certain manner. It is a prerequisite of this sort of interpretation that the subject of the PI sentence should be understood as making a major contribution to the course or outcome of the action exercised upon it. 'Psychological' verbs such as those in (21) are indicative of a state which is more dependent on the person who experiences that state than on the person/thing towards which that state is directed. Similarly, the question of whether or not savings can be withdrawn ((22a)) is likely to be dependent on factors other than the inherent nature of the savings themselves. Contrast (16) and (22b): (16) says that the window is liable to break even though you are doing something to it which is not calculated to break it, and which you do not intend to break it. It would clearly be absurd, on this rendering of the construction, to suggest that, in (22b), the rock buns are liable to be eaten even though the eater has no intention of eating them. However, it is interesting to find the following newspaper example, about a cook turned specialist butcher:

    27. He approaches his new craft from the point
        of view of how the meat will eat and how it
        will cook.

Meat generically is there to be eaten, and the focus

of this sentence is on the contribution that the
meat makes to its being eaten (and cooked).

Applying this kind of reasoning to (23), for
instance, we might say that the task of selling
books involves a number of factors, prominent among
which might be the interest level of the book, the
salience of its cover, etc. In other words, there
are inherent properties of the book which contribute
to the task of selling it. Buying books is a rather
different kind of task - you need to find the book,
have the money, etc. - and the inherent properties
of the book contribute little to this task. This is
not a totally convincing account: sentences such as
(28) do not seem to differ naturally on that basis:

    28. a. That book sells at eight pounds
         b. *That book buys at eight pounds

EXERCISE 3

We have a hypothesis that the subject of a PI
sentence is understood as having an effect on the
way that the action may be carried out on itself.
Does this hypothesis work for the other examples we
have looked at, or for other sentences that you can
think of? Is there any more plausible hypothesis
that you can think of?

2.5. THE GRADABLE NATURE OF OBJECT-DELETION

As we have seen, some verbs which are normally
transitive may occur without an object. But there
appear to be qualitative differences between
different uses without objects - e.g. a verb such as
write or swallow can quite freely be used
intransitively, whereas a verb such as chop, as we
have seen, cannot. Chop, though, would work in a
context where people are discussing how to
distribute the task of disposing of pieces of a
felled tree:

    29. I'll chop

But by no means all verbs will occur in such
contexts: even if we imagine two villains plotting
to kill an old age pensioner and run off with her
life savings, this does not redeem the grammatical
status of:

    30. *I'll murder

But even murder is not irremediably transitive: a
generic use may well be acceptable:

    31. He'll lie, steal, murder - anything to

further his ambitions

There are, of course, verbs which could not normally be used intransitively at all - e.g. <u>attempt</u>, <u>subject</u>, <u>undergo</u>. Given the expressive possibilities inherent in language, however, it would be foolish to claim that even such verbs could never be used intransitively.

Several different classes of verbs are apparent in this gradation of object-deletion. Some verbs may in fact require no object semantically: <u>swallow</u> appears to be such a case - if you swallow something there is a physical object which started off in your mouth and ended up on the way to your stomach. If you just swallow, there is not necessarily any extraneous object associated with the action. (Do you need saliva to swallow? If someone developed a model of the human throat we might say it could swallow even in the absence of salivary glands.) Other verbs which could conceivably be of this class are <u>kick</u>, <u>bite</u> and <u>watch</u>.

A second class of verbs semantically require an object, but the general nature of possible objects is predictable from the class of verb. <u>Write</u>, <u>read</u>, <u>eat</u>, etc. come in this class. A third class has less restricted objects, but the interpretation of intransitive uses is artificially restricted. E.g. with a verb such as <u>visit</u>, its use as a simple verb phrase is very odd, but in a more elaborated structure it is quite acceptable:

32. a. ??John visited
    b. John went visiting

But the understood object cannot be **any** object of <u>visit</u> - e.g. it cannot relate to something like the following sentence:

33. John visited the National Gallery when he was in London

Rather it refers to functional visiting, e.g. of a doctor to his patients, or of someone to his relatives or friends while on holiday.

Sentence (29) above (with <u>chop</u>) makes use of contextual cues to reconstitute the object. This also occurs with, for instance, exam papers or instructions on tins, bottles, etc.:

34. Translate
35. Stand in a pan of boiling water and simmer for five minutes

(which could be rather painful if not interpreted as object-deletion!) The understood object in such cases is always present with the instructions, and unlikely to give rise to uncertainty. Note that such instructions sound very odd if they are embedded in

a larger syntactic context:
  36. ??Go to the library and translate
  'Generic' use also makes intransitivity more
palatable - e.g., still on <u>translate</u>:
  37. He can write essays and talk fluently in
    both Russian and Swahili but he can't translate
(31) above is another example. 'Generic' is used
here in the sense that a propensity to act in a
certain way is referred to. Note also that <u>murder</u>
carries within itself an inherent evaluative
component - soldiers, for instance, do not murder,
except when they are off duty. This generic use of
object-deleting verbs relates them to PI constructions, which also have generic meaning. I suspect
that these can also be graded in terms of how freely
they occur, but this is closely bound up with the
question of which adverbial modifiers can be used in
PI constructions, and which PI verbs can be used
without adverbial modifiers - this is an exceedingly
complex question.
  A final note on this set of constructions: if
we anticipate slightly by including the passive
construction, I believe that we can formulate a set
of class-inclusion relations which have ergative
verbs as a subset of those verbs which can occur in
a PI construction, these in turn being a subset of
those verbs which can occur in the passive, which
form a subset of transitive verbs (in some sense),
themselves one of the major subsets of verbs in
general. The fact that ergative verbs are on the
whole fairly frequent suggests that ergative use of
verbs is a type of 'frozen' PI construction; passive
is, to a degree, a purely formal operation on verbal
constructions in English, and not in its central
core subject to the same kinds of semantico-
pragmatic constraints as the PI construction. It can
therefore be seen as a natural gradation which
relates these constructions to each other.

2.6. TRANSITIVITY AND CASE GRAMMAR

It can be seen that there is a range of properties
which determine the grammatical behaviour of verbs
in the area of transitivity. There are different
approaches which may be taken to the description of
this diversity, and in particular, the approaches
taken by lexicographers and theoretical linguists
will be different. The lexicographer will wish to
represent the various possibilities of use as fully
as possible given limitations of space. Ideally

there would be an example of each type of use, but space seldom allows that. In practice, some variant of the transitive-intransitive distinction is likely to be made use of, either globally, for all meanings of a verb (as in the <u>Concise Oxford Dictionary</u>), or for each individual use of a verb (as in the <u>Collins English Dictionary</u>, for example). More refined classifications exist (e.g. in the <u>Longman Dictionary of Contemporary English</u>), but the lexicographer can also choose whether to incorporate transitivity properties into the definitions he is using (e.g. pseudo-intransitives are often given their own sub-heading in dictionaries). A maximally elegant classificatory schema may not be the best way of conveying the range of use of a particular construction, and the lexicographer may quite legitimately choose to use a variety of techniques to convey grammatical information. (Does anyone **use** the grammatical information in the Longman dictionary?)

By contrast, the theoretical linguist will want to ask questions relating to the status of various transitivity properties; are they semantically determined, partly one and partly the other, or determined by other factors? If semantics comes into it, what form of semantic representation appears relevant? And so on.

The previous sections of this chapter have certainly suggested that semantic considerations are relevant to some extent. So the question of type of semantic representation obviously becomes important. In particular, the most obvious candidate for an appropriate means of representation is some variant of what is usually known as **case grammar.** In common with many other approaches to syntax, case grammar categorises verbs in terms of the types of noun phrase they occur with (obligatorily or optionally) in sentences. But case grammar talks not in terms of 'subjects', 'objects', 'adjuncts', etc. but in terms of the **semantic roles** ('cases') that noun phrases have. On this basis it claims to be able to predict certain aspects of the grammatical behaviour of verbs. A verb such as <u>cut</u> is therefore described not as occurring with a subject and an object, but as occurring with an Agent and a Patient (often called Object(ive) - its semantic status is indicated by the capital letter!). Any verb which occurs with an Agent and a Patient will, in its typical form, have the Agent as subject and the Patient as object. So the grammatical form of a sentence such as

38. John cut the wood

follows from the semantic information that cutting

involves an Agent acting on a Patient.

A more ingenious aspect of the treatment of transitivity properties in case grammar emerges in the treatment of ergative verbs. Break, for instance, is like cut in that it may involve an Agent and a Patient, but unlike cut in that the Agent is not a necessary role in an event of breaking. Things break spontaneously, without an Agent to contribute to the act. A case grammar will therefore characterise break as occurring with an obligatory Patient and an optional Agent. (Note that this type of characterisation is intended to be **semantic**, so elliptical constructions will still show the same case structure as non-elliptical constructions.) When both Agent and Patient occur, the same types of process apply as with cut, and in the neutral form of the verb (i.e. not the passive) the Agent will be subject and the Patient object. But when the Agent role is not present, the Patient, being the only case form present, will be the subject as, at least in English, the subject is the obligatory NP position in sentences. Ergative properties therefore follow naturally from this means of representation. How neat!

Unfortunately, the promise shown by case grammar appears to be fulfilled only in a relatively small number of instances. Three problems are relevant to the concerns of this chapter:

A. There is a complex set of questions associated with the difference between Agents, Instruments, and other things we might wish to claim are involved in performing actions of various sorts. We can break a window with a hammer, say; but a gust of wind could also break a window, as could the contraction of the window frame, someone's carelessness and so on. Do all of these - the wind, the carelessness, the hammer, John, etc. - all have the same semantic role? Within the framework of case grammar we need to be able to provide answers to such questions, and yet it is by no means clear that they are useful questions to ask. Given a range of factors which may be 'causally involved' in an action, to use Fillmore's phrase, the possible interactions of these factors are more likely to follow from facts about the interaction of objects and forces in the 'real world' rather than from any specifically linguistic factors. Whatever case grammar is, it must not become a typology of the world.

B. The facts illustrating case grammar that are presented here involve a highly restricted range of verbs; this is true of the case grammar literature

in general. If we renounce such a highly selective
mode of analysis and start to look relatively
randomly at English verbs, it becomes much less
clear how we would analyse the semantic roles
associated with a large number of verbs. Agent and
Patient are fairly clear, it seems: verbs of mental
experience or perception (e.g. think, enjoy, see)
can be analysed as involving a case relation such as
Experiencer. But what case relations are involved in
verbs such as meet, owe, involve, participate, etc.?
I do not think I am exaggerating the problems; look
in some part of a dictionary and start providing
case 'frames' for verbs, and you will find that
there are many unclear cases. There is another
factor which comes into play when a wider range of
verbs is looked at: there may be ideas which provide
interesting correspondences and apparent insights,
but which turn out to be hard to generalise. E.g. in
one of this papers, Fillmore claims that a set of
verbs like hit (verbs of surface contact) differs
systematically from verbs like break in a way that
is explicable by claiming that the objects of these
verbs are not Patients, but rather Locatives. The
clearest illustrations of this possibility come from
constructions such as He hit her on the nose or He
banged on the door. But a whole host of problems
arise given such an account - why do these verbs not
have complements of overtly locative form? and what
are we to think of such sentences as
     39. He hit the ball over the fence
which do contain a locative constituent, but where
the relationship between hitting and its object is
not thereby altered? It seems plausible to argue
that the treatment of such undoubted generalisations
within case grammar fails time and again quite
simply because the descriptive semantic vocabulary,
being limited to case labels, is impoverished.
C. Ergative verbs just happen to be one of the
favourite examples of case grammarians. But the
other phenomena we have looked at would pose rather
more serious problems if a case grammarian wanted to
deal with them in similar ways. Admittedly this
might not be necessary: as already pointed out, the
difference between simple ergative use, as in The
window broke, and pseudo-intransitive use, as in The
window breaks easily, is that the PI form suggests
an Agent is needed to do the breaking, while the
ergative form does not presuppose an Agent. One of
the problems with 'object-deleting' verbs is that
they manifest a rather subtle gradation between uses

where a Patient is presupposed, and one where it isn't.

But even looking at ergative verbs, case grammar falls down if it is intended as being anything more than a convenient notation (and the claims made by case grammarians are much, much more ambitious than that). If we assume that case grammar effectively encapsulates the difference between verbs like break and cut, it still provides nothing remotely like a semantic basis for the grammatical differences which exist between these verbs. It is only when we know the idiosyncratic lexical specification of each verb that we can tell how it behaves syntactically - but this is hardly surprising given that it is precisely that information which is encoded in a case grammar formula. It should be obvious that the suggestions of a semantic nature made in earlier sections of this chapter are intended to go some way towards giving an explicit semantic characterisation of the different classes of verbs involved in these different constructions. The difference between, for instance, those verbs which allow PI variants and those which do not appears to relate to the situations naturally associated with the actions specified by the verb, but not to such things as the case specification of verbs. In terms of the phenomena considered in this chapter, then, the descriptive framework of case grammar is not of much help in specifying relevant classes of verbs. (It is not outstandingly helpful in other areas, either, to my mind, but that is another argument.)

READING - CHAPTER 2

One recent work which goes over the subject matter of this chapter in great detail is D. J. Allerton Valency and the English Verb, London: Academic Press, 1982; the same sort of issues are raised in chapter 6 of P. H. Matthews Syntax, Cambridge 1981. You might find it interesting to compare the different approaches. More theoretically committed works relevant to this include the systemic approach of M. Halliday 'Notes on transitivity and theme' Journal of Linguistics 3 and 4, 1967-8 and the variant of Extended Standard Theory Transformational Grammar espoused by J. S. Bowers The Theory of Grammatical Relations, Cornell, 1981. All of these works, especially the last two, should be read with considerable scepticism. For work in case grammar,

the most accessible and straightforward work is by
Fillmore - e.g. 'The case for case' in E. Bach and
R. Harms (eds) <u>Universals in Linguistic Theory</u>, New
York: Holt Rinehart, 1968. But there are many other
proposals of interest in slightly different versions
of case grammar - e.g. the 'localist' theory of John
Anderson <u>The Grammar of Case</u>, Cambridge, 1971. The
data on frequency of English verbs comes from T.
West <u>A General Service List of English Words</u> New
York.

Chapter Three

FUNCTIONS OF THE PASSIVE

In the extensive literature on passives in English, the 'typical' active-passive pair is usually of the following type:
1. a. Mary beat John
   b. John was beaten by Mary
There is a further type of passive sentence, the 'short' passive:
2. John was beaten
One very common approach to passives such as (2) is to define them as derivative of 'long' passives such as (1b). We shall not be concerned here with the theoretical issues involved in such an approach. (Like many other simple positions held at an early stage of the development of transformational grammar, this one has become more complex and less amenable to interpretation in terms of relationships between sentences.) It needs to be recognised, however, that any conclusion to the effect that (1b) is a more 'normal' type of passive than (2) would be quite mistaken; any counts that have been done (fairly systematically by Svartvik, less so by Givón and myself) have shown that many types of text show a proportion of around four short passives to one long passive. Overall, short passives constitute between seventy and eighty percent of passives in large corpora of texts. Of course, particular types of language use reveal different proportions of short to long passives, and indeed of passives to non-passives. Passives in general, and long passives in particular, are relatively infrequent in imaginative prose (novels, etc.) and in informal conversation, while informative prose and planned academic conversation contain a higher proportion of both passives in general and long passives in particular.
It is therefore clear enough that we cannot define passives as conforming to the canonical

pattern of (1b), at least for our purposes. (If you assume the level of abstraction allowed in many transformational approaches, then this might of course be possible). Rather, we shall define something as a passive if it meets two conditions: firstly, it must contain a 'past participle' not dependent on the auxiliary <u>has</u>, and secondly, the subject (or understood subject) must be interpretable in the same way as the object of the corresponding active verb. This definition will need to be modified slightly to cope with the problems posed in the next chapter, but it will serve for the moment. One further point can be made about 'long' passives such as (1b). In the overwhelming majority of cases, the agent of such a passive sentence is expressed with the preposition <u>by</u> and a noun phrase. However, it has been argued, with varying degrees of plausibility, that other prepositions too can occur as agents of the passive construction:

3. a. I am empowered, <u>under</u> the act of 1948, to make an inspection of the premises
   b. Appleby was puzzled <u>before</u> this somewhat incoherent vein

(These examples are from Svartvik; many native speakers of English appear puzzled before a sentence like (3b)). Other prepositions also occur in passive-like constructions:

4. a. He's worried <u>about</u> it
   b. No cure is known <u>to</u> man
   c. I was surprised <u>at</u> his aggressiveness
   d. He was concerned <u>with</u> other things
   e. The admission was contained <u>in</u> a letter

The question of whether these prepositions are expressions of passive 'agent' is a moot one. They will be more like passive agents if they can be replaced with <u>by</u>:

5. a. He's worried by it
   b. I was surprised by his aggressiveness
   c. *The admission was contained by a letter

Such substitution may be felt to change the meaning in some sentences, and not so much in others. Some of the participles in constructions like (4) may not be genuinely verbal in character (cf. chapter 5), and hence they may not involve genuine passive constructions. There is also the question of whether the same preposition can be made use of in the active version:

6. a. The door was opened with a key
   b. They opened the door with a key
   c. *His wife concerned him with other things

As the only clear cases of passive agent are those with by, I shall limit myself to those cases in this chapter (but cf. chapter 5 for more discussion). In many languages other than English, passive-like constructions are 'deviant' in the sense that their use is highly restricted and infrequent. This is not so in English, which has an astonishing range of passive constructions, and where they are extremely frequent in at least some types of text. If we compare the use of passive sentences with active transitive sentences (of which passives are usually a variant), passives range from around 5% (in novels and relatively conversational English) up to 50% (in academic prose, etc.) In specific styles, passives may even be more frequent than actives; a quick count of a page of University regulations (p105 of the University of Essex 1980-1 calendar) yields 14 passive clauses and 6 active transitive clauses; 10 of the passives are long passives. Abstracts of scientific articles also tend to abound in passives (in many cases, because of specific instructions to use the passive).

3.2. POSSIBLE DETERMINANTS OF THE PASSIVE

It should be intuitively clear that the active and passive variants are not typically used in exactly the same ways, and that it makes sense to talk about the variants as being determined by several factors. There is no problem about defining in general terms the motivation for the short passive form; agents may be omitted because they are obvious, because they are unknown, because tact or modesty forbids mention of them. Whatever the reason, they may be omitted, and, given that English does not allow subjectless sentences (or at least, formal English does not), the short passive form is virtually required in such contexts. In section 5 we shall look in rather more detail at the possible reasons for omitting mention of the agent; for the moment we shall be satisfied with the fact that the agent is omitted.

It is rather less obvious why full passives should occur. While a short passive is the only way to omit what would have been the subject in the active sentence, all full passives (with minor exceptions which we shall discuss in the next chapter) have corresponding active sentences which could in principle be used perfectly well in their place. There is a very small number of cases where the syntactic structure of a subordinate clause, or certain elements in a main clause, virtually requires that passive be used rather than active:

7.a. The organisers have arranged for the hall at Blackpool to be filled exclusively by tailors' dummies

   b. ... shareholders, led by Stock and Co.

(both newspaper examples). (7b) could, of course, be expanded into an active paraphrase, albeit a rather unnatural one:

7. c. ?shareholders, whom Stock and Co. lead

The peculiarity of (7a) is the adverb <u>exclusively</u>, which appears to be possible in this type of use mainly before prepositional phrases. A further problem is that passives with root modals (i.e. those denoting permission, obligation, etc.) or certain adverbs relating to the subject will involve clear differences in meaning between the active and passive forms:

8. a. The doctor must examine John now

   b. John must be examined by the doctor now

Such cases could only account for a tiny minority of the occurrences of passive, and are not of any great systematic significance. It is occasionally maintained that passive is used to preserve identity of the subject in a sentence such as:

9. He died and was buried in the churchyard beside his wife

This may be true, but raises the question of why the subject **should** be the same for both clauses; it is not unnatural to say:

10. He died and they buried him in the churchyard beside his wife

There is, however, a tendency for the order of NPs in a sentence to occur in a particular 'canonical' order, and we can compare sentences and conclude that one is more 'natural' than another. An example of this is that it appears quite general to prefer an order in which animate, or human, noun phrases, precede other noun phrases. (As is often claimed, active transitive sentences typically have human subjects.) Compare the two variants of (11), contextualised in a situation where someone has just rushed into his place of work and is talking to his colleagues:

11. a. Guess what's happened: a bus has just run a man down

   b. Guess what's happened: a man has just been run down by a bus

English speakers find (11b) more natural than (11a), even though both variants are 'saying the same thing', and there are no contextual factors favouring either order (cf. section 3). Further support for the role of 'humanness' in passive is provided by a class of verbs which require animate, and usually human, objects - e.g. <u>frighten</u>, <u>dismay</u>, <u>delight</u>, <u>shock</u>, <u>astonish</u>, etc. These verbs appear to have an altogether greater likelihood of occurring in the passive form, and often sound much more natural in that form than they do in the active:

12. a. A report in the paper disturbed him
    b. He was disturbed by a report in the paper.

Note, however, that Svartvik observed a strong correlation between passives and **inanimate** subjects - see section 4 of this chapter for discussion.

Similarly, length appears to play a role in the use of the passive, as there is a well-attested tendency for long noun phrases to occur towards the end of sentences. The tendency of passive agents to be long was noted by Svartvik. A sentence such as (13) would be most odd in the active:

13. Profitability will be depressed by weak demand at home and abroad, by worsening competitiveness and increasing cost pressures

It is obviously possible to paraphrase this with an active sentence; in particular, dislocated sentences are quite common to convey this sort of thing:

14. Weak demand at home and abroad, worsening competitiveness and increasing cost pressures - all of these things will depress profitability

There are many more sentence types where the length of the agent is by no means so clearly a source of unnaturalness in the active, but where the passive tends to be used all the same. One of the most striking observations made by Svartvik is that more than half of the animate agents in his corpus were coordinate noun phrases. It seems that coordination is one of the major determinants of 'length' in the required sense.

Slightly less clearly, the use of the passive also appears to be influenced by the definiteness or indefiniteness of the noun phrases which occur in it. Compare the following sentences:

15. a. A young man threw the bomb at her
    b. The young man threw a bomb at her
    c. The bomb was thrown at her by a young man
    d. A bomb was thrown at her by the young man

If you share my intuitions (and many people do!) you will find (b) and (c) more natural than (a) or (d); the order definite-indefinite is favoured. Compare Svartvik (p129) "In agentful clauses, subjects tend to have definite and count nouns, and agents to have indefinite and mass nouns."

3.3. FUNCTIONAL SENTENCE PERSPECTIVE

There is a further factor which is relevant to the use of the passive, and which needs some introduction. It is sometimes called by the useful term 'Functional sentence perspective' - useful because, being a mistranslation from the Czech, it is totally meaningless and therefore unlikely to be misleading. It was an early insight of the 'Prague school' of linguistics that in the Slavonic languages (Russian, Czech, Serbo-Croat, etc.) which have a high degree of freedom of word order, sentence-initial position tends to be used for words or phrases which are, loosely speaking, 'given' or 'predictable' from previous linguistic material, or from the context of utterance, while 'new', less predictable information tended to appear later. These positions were called 'theme' and 'rheme' respectively, and are often used interchangeably, or with only relatively subtle distinctions, with dichotomies such as 'topic-comment', 'presupposition-focus', etc. Even in Slavonic languages the situation is a lot more complex than this; in other languages, where the word order may not be so flexible, the linguistic correlates of thematicity are often more complex, but there is still a tendency in many languages for initial position to correlate with what is 'given'. Some linguists talk of passive sentences being derived from active sentences by a 'movement rule'; others talk of them merely as alternative sentence types with an order of constituents different from that of an active transitive sentence. Whichever perspective we adopt, the choice of a passive sentence can be seen as fitting in with the requirement that thematic material occur at the beginning of the sentence.
    The general idea behind this is that what is 'given' provides some point of contact with previous discourse, setting the scene for some novel piece of information which the speaker wants to impart:
    16. Last night I met my uncle Boris; he said he
        was going to disinherit me
In the second sentence, the first he is given, and the theme, while the content of his speech is the significant information contained in that sentence.

If all the information in a sentence (at least in a sentence which is embedded in some sort of discourse) were new, and if this were typical of the structure of sentences, then discourse would simply be an amalgam of unrelated utterances, hardly worthy of the name 'connected speech' :

    17. Last night I met my uncle Boris. The structure of British universities is quite different from that of American universities

For virtually any pair of sentences such as those in (17), it is possible to invent a discourse in which that juxtaposition makes a certain amount of sense. If my uncle Boris is a British professor and I am talking to an American, then (17) makes a certain amount of sense as an introduction to the fact that my uncle Boris is a man of some standing in the university he is in, and not just any old teacher. However, the point that I am making still stands; a discourse may develop more than one strand of thought virtually simultaneously, to bind them together at a later stage, but a discourse cannot consist of a mere sequence of thematically unrelated utterances. This is one of the basic motivations of the theme-rheme distinction.

    I do not aim to provide anything approaching a complete exposition of functional sentence perspective. But, if only to maintain its plausibility, it is necessary to add some correctives to this oversimple picture. Theme is not necessarily given information in the sense that it has already been mentioned in discourse, nor is rheme always new information in the sense that it has nowhere been mentioned. Some Prague school theorists have preferred to look at this distinction as a scalar one - involving gradations of 'communicative dynamism'. Those things which have little communicative dynamism (i.e. which are thematic) tend to be:

- phrases which are given in the sense specified above
- locative or temporal settings of situations
- semantically vacuous (or nearly so) verbs (e.g. be, arise, etc. - verbs of existence or coming into existence)
- words used for speaker evaluation of the situation described (e.g. unfortunately, possibly).

Greater communicative dynamism (i.e. rhematic status) is possessed by:

- new information, particularly that which bears a grammatical relation to the verb (especially objects and indirect objects)
- semantically highly meaningful verbs

      - given information which is not readily predictable.

      This final notion can be illustrated with a simple example; Tom, Dick and Harry are playing golf in the garden, and suddenly a golf ball sails through the greenhouse roof. Father comes out and says 'Who did it?', and is told 'Harry did it'. <u>Harry</u> is given information - he is one of the three suspects - but is also the rheme (cf. the intonational prominence he is given) because he does not emerge with any predictability from the context.

      The distinction between semantically empty verbs and highly meaningful verbs can also be illustrated simply, given the following mini-discourses:

    18. I was just sitting down to enjoy 'Coronation Street' when suddenly the telephone rang

    19. I was just sitting down to enjoy 'Coronation Street' when suddenly the telephone made a funny noise

If you read (18) and (19) aloud, I think you will find that the most natural reading of (18) is one where <u>rang</u> is virtually unstressed, while <u>telephone</u> is quite heavily stressed. By contrast, the phrase <u>made</u> a <u>funny noise</u> receives much heavier stress in (19). The motivation for this is not hard to see; we are not accustomed to telephones doing many things other than ring, so that if the telephone did something, it is exceedingly likely that what it did would be ring. But telephones do not normally make funny noises, so the information that it did is significant. Obviously <u>ring</u> could not be replaced by many other words with the same function. But for a whole range of verbs we would wish to stress them if they occurred in the context of (19) - e.g. <u>exploded</u>, <u>fell</u> <u>off</u> the <u>shelf</u>, <u>melted</u>, etc. Note that this can be overriden by contextual factors. If I am telling a story where everything in the house emits funny noises, then (19) would most likely be uttered with the same intonation as the normal reading of (18). Note that the term 'stress' here is the subject of much debate, and many people prefer to use 'accent' for types of salience above the level of the word. It seems likely that pitch adjustments are the most direct physical correlate of this type of salience: however, I suspect that most speakers of English will find it easier to recognise impressionistic terms such as 'stress' or 'accent' than 'objective' factors such as pitch, amplitude, duration, etc., which are notoriously difficult to perceive, even for trained phoneticians.

      To get back to the relevance of FSP to the

passive, not only does it seem likely that subjects of passive sentences are going to be 'given', but there is also a connection between the thematic status of a noun phrase and its definiteness and length. Definite NPs are by no means always given, but there is a strong tendency in that direction, and if something is given in discourse or context, it is unlikely to need a particularly long NP to refer to it unambiguously. A relative clause, for instance, is used to help the hearer identify the thing referred to in a NP: if a NP is genuinely thematic, then such assistance will probably be unnecessary. It may be that there is also a connection between FSP and humanness, in that, as is frequently observed, human beings are more likely to make up the topic of conversation among other human beings than are inanimate objects.

3.4. SOURCES OF DATA

In some areas of syntax we can be fairly sure that our intuitions are giving us a satisfactory account of the range of data we need. If we want to know about the use of time adverbs with the present perfect in English, we are more likely to find out by observing that speakers of standard English reject sentences such as (20) than we are by discovering that somebody's novels do not contain instances of the use of this kind of construction:

    20. *John has died yesterday

(Of course, if somebody's novels **do** contain sentences like this, then that is a different matter.) But the fact remains that native speakers of English do disagree on the acceptability of certain types of sentence (as we shall see more clearly in chapter 5). Moreover, while we can ask of (20) whether it is acceptable or not, the sorts of questions we were asking in section 3.2. were rather different: is this sentence more natural than that one? It is by no means clear what that means. And when we bring the acceptability of discourses into range, it is also not clear whether the intuitions we have are at all reliable.

    Each type of problem may require distinct means of overcoming it. However, with a construction as frequent as the passive, there is little problem in collecting 'real' language data on which we can test the hypotheses of previous sections. Admittedly there may be problems of style, genre, etc. - the high incidence of passives in abstracts of scientific articles, for instance, could hardly justify us in drawing conclusions about the passive in English in general. However, what is at issue here is not the frequency of the passive but the functions of the passive when it does occur. It seems reasonable to assume, at least as a first approximation, that the passive fulfils roughly the same functions - even if not in the same proportions - in different types of texts. Variations in frequency might follow either from differences in available linguistic resources, or from differences in characteristic functional requirements for different types of text. The lower incidence of passives in colloquial spoken English, for instance, can be put down to the greater functional load carried by intonational factors in that register, rather than to any fundamentally different syntactic properties that it might have. I.e. when intonational prominence is available as an indicator of the communicative load which characterises an element, it is likely to be less necessary to have recourse to variant syntactic constructions to express the same thing. Furthermore, if different types of text differ characteristically in terms of complexity of sentences, then those uses of the passive which serve to promote parallelism in conjoined or subjoined clauses might be expected to occur only in more complex styles.

The basic corpus of data to be analysed here comes from a history book (Asa Briggs *Victorian Cities*, Penguin). I selected the first hundred passives of any type in the text (excluding participial/adjectival use without agent), and the next hundred full passives (i.e. excluding short passives, without agents). Twenty two of the first hundred passives are full passives, giving me a corpus of 78 short passives and 122 full passives. In addition, I have, less systematically, collected examples of the passive from informal conversations, recordings of spontaneous talk on the radio, etc., and will use this data where there appears to be some significant difference from the more formal text. (These examples will be marked (S) in the following section.)

It is worth pointing out that there is a certain fuzziness in the notion of 'passive', under most definitions. The two major problems are (i) that the past participle is not always obviously passive (even when not following have), most clearly in sentences such as (21a), but also in (21b) and (21c), for example:
21 a. He's gone

    b. Most of philosophy is posed upon these
       conundrums (S)
    c. She wasn't thrilled with the idea (S)
(ii) the notion of 'agent' is not clear: firstly, as
mentioned earlier, because not all 'agents' are
marked with <u>by</u> (cf. (21c) above); secondly, because
not all <u>by</u>-phrases are obviously agents:
    22. fuchsias which have been produced by
       rooting and cutting (S)
I have also counted as passives constructions which
involve passives in relative clauses, complement
clauses with deleted subjects, <u>there</u>-constructions,
etc., even though these do not have all the elements
of a simple passive sentence.

3.5. SOME RESULTS OF THE ANALYSIS OF THE CORPUS

The use of the short passive can be classified in
terms of the reasons for omitting the agent. I shall
mention six of these in order of their frequency of
occurrence in 'my' text, plus a seventh which is
apparently characteristic only of speech.
    A. The agent is known, but is either too complex
to specify briefly, or is irrelevant to the point
being made:
    23. The first electric railway was opened in
       1890
    24. A Nuisance Removal Act had been passed as
       early as 1846
    25. Eastbourne and Hastings were also described
       at this time as 'isolated suburbs of London'
    B. The agent is too diffuse to specify at all:
    26. We know relatively little of how Victorian
       cities were actually built
    27. In London large quantities of strawberries
       were grown in Deptford and Camberwell in the
       1830s
    28. The word 'city' itself has been used in so
       many different senses
    C. The agent is taken to refer to **anyone** con-
cerned or interested; in this use, a modal verb
usually occurs:
    29. Some of the best pictures of cities are to
       be found in George Meason's Official Illus-
       trated Railway Guide Books
    30. The two sides of the picture must be taken
       together in assessing Victorian experience
    31. If the detailed study of Victorian cities is
       not pursued at this perilous moment of time ...
    D. Authorial modesty - i.e. the agent is the

author.
  32. Other cities might well have been included:
      some of the cities included might have been
      left out
  33. There is, however, another difficulty which
      must be mentioned
This use tends not to occur in spoken language,
although there is a use of the passive where the
speaker is keen to avoid direct responsibility:
  34. It wasn't done intentionally, dear   (S)
  E. The passive expresses a state of affairs, and
does not suggest an action for which there must have
been an agent:
  35. Many of the most illuminating sources are
      buried away in the most unlikely places
  36. Perhaps their outstanding feature was hidden
      from public view - their hidden network of pipes
      and drains and sewers
  F. A frequency adverb is used which effectively
expresses a rather indeterminate notion of agent:
  37. Railways were also often believed, like
      cities, to be symbols of 'democracy'
  38. The term 'suburbia' became increasingly
      associated with the flight from the worst parts
      of the city
(E.g. in (38) increasingly conveys exactly the same
thing as the agent phrase by an increasing number of
people.)
  G. A category which does not occur in the basic
written corpus (although for no very obvious reason)
is the omission of the agent because it is obvious:
  39. When you see the whole of this structure ...
      devoted to puzzles and puns, you don't really
      feel it's being put to proper use   (S)
  40. a clump of it which she thought had been
      disposed of last winter (i.e. by her)   (S)
      It should be clear that this classification is
to an extent arbitrary, particularly in the division
between A and B. Nor is it exhaustive (although it
does exhaust my main corpus): it is possible to use
the short passive where the agent, though specific,
is unknown to the speaker:
  41. John's car has been stolen
This is found in my spoken corpus too, although the
examples are not so clear:
  42. She's had a pot plant given to her   (S)
And further distinctions could of course be drawn: a
sentence such as (43) can be converted into a colloquial active sentence by using the 'they of
officialdom', but it would require a certain amount
of paranoia to do the same with (41):

43. a. The pub across the road has been demolished
    b. They've demolished the pub across the road
44. ?They've stolen John's car

Table 3.1. Numbers (and proportions) of NP uses in a corpus of 122 full passives.

	Subject NP	Agent NP
Given	89 (73%)	25 (20.5%)
New	10 (8%)	97 (79.5%)
Other*	23 (19%)	0
Definite	85 (69.5%)	78 (64%)
Indefinite	14 (11.5%)	44 (36%)
Animate	20 (16%)	61 (50%)
Inanimate	79 (65%)	61 (50%)

---

* The category 'other; includes the it which correlates with an extraposed sentential complement (2 cases - e.g. 'it is thought by many that he is ill') and the relative pronoun (21 cases). Note that these 23 cases are missing from the definiteness and animacy lists, which is why the figures for subject NPs do not add up to 100%.
NB 'Definite' NP is understood as i. a NP beginning with a definite article, ii. a proper name, iii. a personal pronoun

---

Figures for the definiteness, animacy and thematic status of the full passives in this corpus are given in Table 3.1. It can be seen fairly immediately from these figures that definiteness and animacy are not particularly good predictive factors in the choice of the passive construction. By contrast, thematic status seems to be a remarkably strong correlate of subject and agent status. The corpus contains only five sentences with a given agent but a new subject, and 'special factors' appear to be at work in at least some of these:
45. Even liberals were often shocked by the government of almost all American cities

Here the agent is a long NP, the verb is of the special class noted in section 3.2. which are extremely frequently found in the passive, and the intensifier _even_ does not sit happily next to a direct object (shocked even liberals).

46. A house formerly occupied by Cobden was chosen by his trustees as the first house of the university

(incidentally, the trustees are not Cobden's!) I am not at all certain why this should not be in the active, but it may have something to do with avoiding the accumulation of two quite separate long constituents at the end of a sentence.

47. A statue of the Queen ... had been presented to the Council by the Mayor

This is one of many examples where the precise nature of 'thematic' status seems rather unclear. In terms of participants being mentioned in previous discourse, or being implicit in the situation described, there is no doubt that the Council and the Mayor are given, while the statue of Queen Victoria is a piece of new information. However, the context in which this sentence occurs is that of the finishing touches being put to Leeds Town Hall prior to its opening by Queen Victoria: the things that are being discussed are those things which are being put up in the immediate surroundings of the Town Hall. In that context, although the statue itself is mentioned for the first time, the general category of decorative objects is clearly given. It may be that in this sense (47) is not a counterexample.

It is important to stress this point; the notions 'given' and 'new', or 'theme' and 'rheme' are not at all easy to apply in practice; phrases tend to be a little bit of one and a little bit of the other, e.g.:

48. A key role in the victory was played by W. J. Davis, the secretary of the brass workers

It is obvious enough that the victory referred to is given in context; however, not all victories can be said to have 'key roles', so that the NP is partly new, at the very least. But if (48) is considered not so much in terms of whether we really want to call the subject 'given' or 'new', but rather in terms of which NP contains the major informational input to the sentence, it becomes fairly clear, I think, that the agent is 'more important' as new information than the subject. Even looked at from this perspective, the 'rule-governed' nature of this correlation is not as obvious as might be desired, but we are perhaps more likely to get rather closer to an adequate definition of 'theme', etc. if we take this line of thought. It is not easy to be sure whether this difficulty of application is the fault of the theory, or of language. In other words, one possibility is that the basic notions of FSP are inadequately developed, and that more work will allow us to elaborate these notions in such a way that these difficulties will be overcome. The alternative is that it is difficult to apply these notions simply because that aspect of language structure is not rigidly determined at all, and the structure of English itself determines the latitude of interpretation we have observed here. Both of these suggestions are plausible to some degree, and there may be some truth in both of them. We are unlikely to be in a position to say that any construct of linguistic theory could not be developed or refined to make it more adequate; on the other hand the relevant facts in this area are sufficiently flexible and variable to suggest that no totally rigid account is likely to provide a close analogue to the facts of linguistic usage.

I have not tabulated length as a factor; this is partly because the relevant notion of 'length' is one which is by no means clear. Counting syllables will not do, for instance. Two things appear to be relevant - the presence of relative clause(s) in a NP, and, most importantly, the question of whether the NP is a list or not. This last factor can be seen in (49):

49. The Leeds police force with its 221 members was to be augmented by 160 from the West Riding, 50 from Bradford, 93 from London ...

The presence of relative or complement clauses is obviously relevant in (50) and (51):

50. It was organised by the Leeds Chamber of Commerce which had been formed in 1851

51. Its impact was strengthened by the fact that the prestige - and wealth - of the majority of Birmingham's most respected families were moving forces behind local dissent

Of course, both of these contain pronouns in their subjects - a mark of givenness.

One other factor which emerges with a certain amount of clarity from the corpus is that animate NPs (which are all human NPs in this corpus) other than personal pronouns appear to show a strong tendency to occur as Agent of the passive, in spite of certain other factors being unfavourable to the use of the passive. (47) is one example of this; there are others:

52. The sense of adventure in local government
    and of increased responsibility were learned
    by Chamberlain not only from advanced Liberals
    like Harris
53. The suggestion was made that a Town Hall
    should be built by the Town Council out of the
    rates
54. ... a tower which had been rejected by the
    Council in February

This appears to contradict the sorts of argument put
forward in section 3.2. about the role of human NPs.
In fact it is not in direct contradiction to that
suggestion: verbs like <u>shock</u> and <u>delight</u> **do** appear
to behave in a rather different way, while sentences
such as (11), where virtually all the information is
new, may obey rather different regularities from the
textually-bound sentences we have been considering.
The generality of the conclusions reached in section
3.2. is misleading; but we would perhaps need to
look at a variety of verb types and a variety of
functional contexts in which animacy was a distinctive feature before we could decide on a question
such as this.

EXERCISE 1

Look at some texts (spoken or written) of a rather
different sort from those I have looked at. Does the
use of the passive in this corpus obey the same
types of constraints as I have mentioned?

EXERCISE 2

I have mentioned some of the criteria by which
'theme' and 'rheme' can be distinguished; try applying these criteria to real data. Are there any
additions or modifications which are necessary to
make the distinction workable?

EXERCISE 3

What devices are available in spoken English which
might be used instead of the passive construction to
thematise NPs, or to alter their salience?

READING - CHAPTER 3

The major quantitative study of the passive is J.
Svartvik <u>On Voice in the English Verb</u>, The Hague:

Mouton, 1966, and there are also useful observations in T. Givón On Understanding Grammar, New York: Academic Press, 1979. There is no really good general account of Functional Sentence Perspective, but many different specific points of view relating to it. Some of these are represented in F. Daneš Papers in Functional Sentence Perspective, The Hague: Mouton, 1976 and in C. N. Li (ed) Subject and Topic, New York: Academic Press, 1976, especially in the article by W. Chafe, which looks at some useful distinctions, although these are by no means above criticism. A recent textbook which promises to fill at least part of this gap in relation to FSP is G. Brown and G. Yule Discourse Analysis, Cambridge, 1983.

Chapter Four

THE RANGE OF THE PASSIVE

There is a view of the passive which holds that it
always relates a sequence of the form
          Subject NP   - Verbal - Object NP - X
(where X can be anything at all, or nothing, and
'Verbal' is a term which includes auxiliaries to the
left of the main verb, and such things as particles
on the right) to a sequence of the form
Former Obj - Passive verbal - X - (by Former Subj)
It is well enough known that this is oversimplistic,
in a number of ways:
- not all active sentences of the form specified
have a passive counterpart (see Exercise 1 below);
- a variety of things can occur in between the
verbal and the object NP of the active sentence
without causing deviance in the corresponding
passive form;
- a very small number of sentence types can only be
passive.
In this chapter most emphasis will be given to cases
where a preposition occurs between a verb and a noun
phrase in the active sentence. But it is worth
briefly considering some of the other cases first.
     We shall, in this chapter and the next, come
across constructions which are characteristically
restricted to the passive. However, these are rather
marginal cases. There is also a small set of verbs
which occur only in the passive - e.g.:
     1. He is rumoured/reputed by his friends to have
                    no chance
These verbs are obviously exceptional; however,
their degree of exceptionality is limited by the
fact that they occur in exactly the same context as
a much larger group of verbs which do have an active
form, but which have no active form corresponding
directly to this use:

EXERCISE 1

Following is a sample of sentences which do not have
a corresponding passive form, although they appear
to have the relevant structural characteristics. In
some cases you may find that there is an acceptable
passive form which deviates in some way from what
might be expected if passive simply involved the
structural changes found in most formulations of the
passive transformation. How would you account for
the fact that these sentences do not have passive
forms?

2. a. John can read Amharic
   b. Poor old Smith kicked the bucket last night
   c. The car holds five adults
   d. Green suits Mary
   e. I prevented anyone from leaving
   f. The book costs five pounds
   g. John shaved himself carefully
   h. He seems a nice chap
   i. Mary makes a good teacher
   j. It fits you perfectly
   k. I held my breath
   l. I saw him come in
   m. This means war!
   n. John outlived the disgrace
   o. It surprised me that he said that
   p. John wants Mary to come
   q. It's raining cats and dogs
   r. He weighs 17 stone
   s. John has that book
   t. The library lacks it
   u. They made it work
   v. A tree overhangs the stream
   w. Jack drives a truck for a living
   x. She helped him get up
   y. John resembles Mary
   z. The train neared the station
   aa. This dress becomes her
   bb. John is a fink
   cc. He survived the accident
   dd. The reason escapes me
   ee. The filming involved a lot of location work

3. He is said/thought/reckoned/claimed/admitted
     by his friends to have no chance
Most of the verbs which occur in this sort of sentence do not have active forms which directly correspond to this pattern (4), although they do have
active forms which convey essentially the same meaning:
4. *His friends say/think/claim/admit him to
     have no chance
5. His friends say/think/reckon/claim/admit that
     he has no chance
Reckon, on my intuitions, is a somewhat marginal
case, intermediate between say and believe (which
occurs in sentences like (4)). There may, therefore,
be some irregularity in this construction; however,
it occurs with such a wide range of verbs of the
relevant semantic class that it does appear to be
quite a productive construction.
     Where a verb is followed by more than one NP,
with or without a preposition, it is rarely possible
to promote the second NP to subject position while
leaving the first NP intact:
6. a. John pinned a brooch onto her jacket
   b. *Her jacket was pinned a brooch onto by
        John
There are some idiomatic combinations, however,
where a passive of this form is quite possible:
7. a. John took advantage of Mary
   b. Mary was taken advantage of by John
8. a. Everyone made fun of John
   b. John was made fun of by everyone
There are other idiomatic combinations which do not
naturally occur in the passive in this way:
9. a. Mary took umbrage at John's manner
   b. *?John's manner was taken umbrage at by
        Mary
There has been a tendency among linguists to dismiss
this construction by claiming that a sequence such
as take advantage of is merely a complex verb, and
that the passive is really quite regular. Bolinger
(1977) has effectively exploded this approach by
showing that the construction is much more productive than is often allowed for. Bolinger's examples
often sound quite unacceptable to me, but sufficiently many of them are good for his point to seem
quite valid. Bolinger gives examples such as:
10. He has been burned, stuck pins in, beheaded
     - all in effigy, of course
11. To be whispered such dirty innuendoes about
     was enough to break any girl's heart
A useful exercise would be to go through Bolinger's

examples, grading them for their acceptability (independently of Bolinger's own grading), and giving constructive criticism of the factors Bolinger claims to be relevant. Naturally such sentences rarely crop up in texts: but they may on occasions - cf. these examples from spontaneous speech:

12. This can be made sense of in the following way
13. That needs to be done a little more work on
14. The health workers appear to be being made an example of

Even in the shakiest of examples it is quite clear that some constraints need to be obeyed. Most clearly, the first object in these constructions must not be definite (unless the construction is idiomatic):

15. a. ??He was thrown stones at
    b. *He was thrown the stone at
16. ?They were read the riot act to by their teacher

EXERCISE 2

Look at a range of idiomatic expressions of an appropriate form and determine which pattern as in (7)-(8) and which as in (9). Is there any recognisable basis for this distinction? A starting list:

    have regard to   give vent to
    take pains with   keep tabs on
    make short work of   work wonders with

4.2. PREPOSITIONS AND PARTICLES

Most of this chapter concerns the possibility of passive form for sentences with a verb followed by a preposition:

17. a. Someone needs to look at the carburettor
    b. The carburettor needs to be looked at by someone

Before doing this, however, it is necessary to draw a distinction between constructions with prepositions and constructions with particles - so-called 'phrasal verbs', which will be looked at separately in chapter 6:

18. a. Everyone should look up this word in the dictionary
    b. This word should be looked up in the dictionary by everyone

Transitive phrasal verbs virtually without exception have passive variants while prepositional verbs are

highly variable in this respect. Failure to distinguish these two apparently similar constructions
would inevitably result in confusion.

The essence of the distinction between prepositional constructions (as in (17)) and phrasal verbs
(as in (18)) is that the preposition in the first
construction makes up a single constituent with the
NP which follows the verb, while the particle in
the phrasal verb construction behaves partly as an
independent constituent and partly as a form
attached to the verb. Four aspects of their
syntactic behaviour (at least) differentiate them
fairly consistently.

A. Particles occur either immediately after the
verb or immediately after the direct object, while
prepositions only occur before the NP to which they
are attached and which they govern:
19. a. *Someone needs to look the carburettor at
    b. Everyone should look this word up
If the direct object is a personal pronoun, only the
preposition may precede it; particles always follow
personal pronoun objects (unless these are heavily
stressed):
20. a. Someone needs to look at it
    b. Someone needs to look up it (not inter-
       pretable as (14b))
B. Particles cannot be separated from the verb
by an adverb, but prepositions can:
21. a. Someone needs to look carefully at the
       carburettor.
    b. *Everyone should look carefully up this
       word
C. Particles can be followed by of when the
phrasal verb is used in the nominal form in -ing.
Prepositions never occur in this context:
22. a. *The looking at of the carburettor is a
       useful exercise
    b. The looking up of this word was a useful
       exercise
Palmer (1974 p218) claims to find (23) acceptable:
23. The running up of the hill was the hardest
       part of the exercise
Relatively few speakers of English appear to agree
with this intuition, as far as I can determine.
D. In coordinate constructions with identical
verbs, it is often possible to delete the second
verb ('Gapping'). The preposition can be left
undeleted in such circumstances, but particles never
can:
24. a. John looked at the carburettor and Bill
       at the fuel pump

        b. *John looked up this word and Bill up
              that one
Using these criteria it should always be possible to
distinguish whether the construction at issue is
prepositional or phrasal. In this chapter only prepositional constructions are being considered.

4.3. APPROACHES TO PREPOSITIONAL PASSIVES

In the literature on prepositional passives, some of
the ideas put forward appear to be purely notation-
al, not substantive; e.g. it has been suggested that
there is a rule which incorporates a preposition as
part of the verb, thereby making it possible to
retain the regularity of the active-passive relation. Unfortunately this is of no help at all, as it
merely shifts the burden from the question of which
verbs passivise to the question of which verbs
undergo the restructuring rule which allows them to
passivise. The gain in simplicity of stating which
active sequences correspond to passive ones is
entirely illusory. Other than proposals such as
this, there are two major classes of suggestions
which have been made in the literature on prepositional passives. The first of the genuine suggestions, made by Bresnan among others, is that the
passive works in constructions where the relationship between the verb and the preposition approaches
idiomaticity. Bresnan notes contrasts such as the
following:
        25. a.   That conclusion was independently
              arrived at by several investigators
            b. *The stadium was simultaneously arrived
              at by several competitors
        26. a. John is looked up to by his students
            b. *The sky was looked up to by the
              sunbathers
There is undoubtedly something to this suggestion.
The sorts of prepositional constructions which are
not altogether happy in the passive construction are
usually those which express very concrete relationships - spatial relations, and others such as
accompaniment, instrumental, etc. More 'abstract'
prepositional meanings tend also to be more readily
compatible with the passive. The notion of 'idiomaticity' is a complex one (see chapter 6 for more
discussion): in relation to this construction I
shall call a verb + preposition combination idiomatic if the verb selects that preposition, and there
is no intuitively clear semantic basis for the

exclusion of other prepositions.

Unfortunately, again as pointed out most forcefully by Bolinger, this is not a necessary criterion for passivisability, as we find contrasts such as the following:

27. a. ?This hill was walked up by John
    b. This hill has been walked up by generations of schoolchildren
28. a. ??That bed was slept on by John Smith
    b. That bed was slept on by Queen Victoria
29. a. ??The city was left by John
    b. The city was left by half of its inhabitants

Of course the oddity of some of these sentences is only relative to the presumed insignificance of John (Smith). It is not just prepositional passives which illustrate this contrast, as we can see from (29). Note that it is the idiomaticity of the verb + preposition combination which is at issue here; if the idiomatic link is between the preposition and its NP, passive is very unlikely:

30. a. The low bridge was driven under by the bus driver
    b. *The influence of drink was driven under by the bus driver

The second suggestion as a criterion for passivisability is that the relevant parameter is whether the NP to be promoted to subject is 'affected' by the action of the verb or not. This is suggested by contrasts such as:

31. a. The flowerbed was walked over by the children
    b. ??The flowerbed was walked over by ants
    c. ??The flowerbed was jumped over by the children

Children walking over a flowerbed are apt to do nasty things to it (to deflower it?); but nothing much is going to be affected if ants walk over a flowerbed, nor if children jump over it without touching it (note also the contrast with jumped all over which suggests that they jumped, but landed on the flowerbed). (27)-(29) are also consistent with this suggestion, as long as we assume, for instance, that association with a famous figure (as in (28a)) marks out an object as being rather special.

Once again this is not a necessary criterion for the possibility of putting a verb in the passive form. There are many simple verbs which passivise but which do not involve an action which affects the object, and this is also true of at least some prepositional constructions:

32.a. The proceedings were watched by some
        children
   b. The book was first read by John
   c. That baby needs to be cleaned up after
        (all the time)
        (passive of '(You) need to clean up after
        that baby (all the time)')
   d. The bridge was sheltered under by some
        tramps
It is not always obvious when the passive subject
can plausibly be considered 'affected'. It has been
claimed, for instance, that <u>live in</u>, when passiv-
ised, acquires extra meaning relating to the affected nature of the subject. In support of such an
assertion we usually find examples such as:
   33. That house looks lived in
However this is quite unsatisfactory: the inference
that the house is in some way affected by being
lived in is really an inference from the verb <u>looks</u>,
which cannot be used appropriately unless there is
some visible sign of the state of affairs characterised by its complement. In a rather more neutral
sentence, as in (34), the inference of affecting
seems quite absent:
   34. a. That house is lived in by the family I
           was telling you about
       b. Many of these second homes are lived in
           for only a few months of the year
Of course you can argue about the degree to which
something is affected or not by an action; that is
part of the unsatisfactory nature of this criterion.
But in terms of relatively straightforward intuitive
notions, (34) could only be at best a marginal
instance of affected passive subject.

4.4. SOME DATA

On the basis of this discussion it seems reasonable
to expect that all verbs which involve an affected
object, all verbs which are idiomatically related to
a following preposition, and of course all verbs
which have both of these features should passivise.
There remains the awkward question of how large a
residue there is - i.e. of how many verb + preposition combinations allow the passive but are neither
affected nor idiomatic. There is little point in
attempting to answer this question with a survey of
texts, as we did in the last chapter. The reason for
this is obviously that the number of occurrences of
any particular verb in even a very large text would

be unlikely to be very great; passives of prepositional verbs are not rare in texts, but they are
not especially frequent either. An added factor
(which must be Somebody's Law) is that the types of
combination which are particularly crucial in distinguishing different hypotheses are always the
rarest in terms of their occurrence in texts. Illuminating real-life examples **do** occur however - cf.
the following newspaper examples:

35. In the Middle Ages, the spa of the
eventually royal town of Bath was gone to by the
sick of all classes
36. 'The Americans like to be sold to, and it's
demonstrable that the selling works'

(35) seems to go against the criteria mentioned here
(and it does strike me as rather an odd sentence).
(36) is interpreted as involving active, pressure
selling, so the passive subject can well be seen as
affected in this instance.

In the absence of large quantities of natural
data, I shall, as a sort of pilot study, select a
number of verbs in a relatively random fashion (open
a dictionary and start enumerating verbs), and
tabulate their compatibility with the prepositions
in, on, from, with, under, for. Why these prepositions? Simply that they provide a reasonable range
of co-occurrence. I then intuit as to whether they
passivise and their status with respect to affected
objects and idiomaticity. This then provides a
corpus of observations on which to test hypotheses.
I present such a (small) corpus in Table 4.1.

There are at least two substantial pitfalls in
this approach. The first is that, as you can see
from (27)-(31), it is not just the verb-preposition
combination which determines whether passivisation
is possible. It is clearly not possible to put in
all permutations of passive subject, prepositional
verb and agent to see if each one is permissible.
That is a complication we shall just have to live
with: I have tried in exercising my intuitions to
allow as passivisable even those verbs which require considerable contextual support. The second
problem is that prepositions are often highly ambiguous; consider the sentence in (37) and the corresponding passives in (38) (slightly modified in an
attempt to make them more plausible):

37. a. He plays for Chipping Sodbury Casuals
    b. They are obviously playing for a draw
    c. He is just playing for time
    d. They play for the honour of representing
       their country

Table 4.1. Some verbs and their co-occurrence with prepositions

in	on	from	with	under	for
paddle	paint A	paddle	paddle	[paddle]	paddle
[paint]	panic	paint	paint	paint	[paint]
panic	pant	[parachute]	parachute	panic	pant
pant	[parade]	parade	[parade]	pant	parachute
parachute	park	part	park	[parachute]	pause
[parade]	part	pass	[part]I	[parade]	pedal
park	[patrol]	pedal	participate	[park]	[perform]
part	pause	percolate	patrol	pass	perish
participate I	pedal	perish	pedal	patrol	petition I
[patrol]	perch	[phone]	persist	pause	phone
pause	[perform]	play	picnic	pedal	pine I
pedal	perish	plummet	play A	peek	[play]
peek	[picnic]	plunge	plead	peer	plead
peep	[pivot]A?	pour	[practise]	[perform]	plump I
[peer]	play A	prance	proceed I	perish	ply I
percolate	ponder I	[preach]	progress	[picnic]	pose I
perform	pounce A/I	[profit]I	push	play	practise
perish	pound A	progress		plunge	pray I
persist I	[prance]	prosper		pour	[prepare]I
picket	[preach]	protrude		prance	press I
[picnic]	prevail A/I			[probe]	[pronounce]
play	prey A/I			[prowl]	provide
plunge	proliferate				publish
[potter]	[prowl]				push I
pour					
prance					
[preach]					
predominate					
prepare					
progress					
proliferate					
prosper					
[prowl]					
pry					
publish					

In each column are the verbs which co-occur with each preposition (remember, not particles).
Underlining indicates that the passive is fine; square bracketing means that it is marginal; nothing means that it is excluded. Verbs suffixed A have affected object, and those with I have an idiomatic link between verb and preposition. (All judgements DAK's.)

38. a. Chipping Sodbury Casuals are played for
by some of the best players in the land
    b. Obviously a draw is being played for
here
    c. Time is being played for by the winning
side
    d. The honour of representing their country
is played for by the whole of the Ruritanian team
Try grading the sentences in (38) for acceptability
(then compare your judgements with mine, which go -
from best to worst - b, a, c, d). I have tried to
take the best possible interpretation in filling in
the table; but if you find my judgements particularly eccentric in any cases, perhaps I had a
different context for the construction in mind.
     With so many qualifications it might be argued
that this type of exercise is not really of great
interest. The response to that is merely to point to
the alternatives. In all the literature on this
subject the overwhelming response has been to consider single pairs of examples, if possible minimal
pairs, such as lie on/rely on, or the two uses of
arrive at (cf. (25) above). The approach of a
linguist like Bolinger is rather different, but
still involves carefully selected examples, carrying
with it the danger that inconvenient types of data
will be missed. I am not knocking either of these
methods as such: but exclusive reliance on either of
them (or on the sampling method adopted here)
clearly misses out potential sources of data.
     What conclusions emerge from the tabulated
display? On the whole the claim that idiomatic and
affected-object verb-preposition constructions
passivise is supported remarkably well. There are a
few slightly problematic cases, however, which,
although not completely unacceptable in the passive,
are very dubious:
39. a. ??The central column is pivoted on by
three arms
    b. ?His mistakes were profited from by his
enemies
    c. ??Money is parted with by Scotsmen only
with great reluctance
    d. ?The match was eagerly prepared for by
the two teams
The status of these sentences as counterexamples
clearly depends on the reliability of their classification as affected-object or idiomatic. As I have
already pointed out, the first is very vague; as we
shall see in chapter 6, in discussing phrasal verbs,
the question of idiomaticity is also problematic.

EXERCISE 3

Try to specify in rather more detail than I have
done what it means for an object to be affected.
You could use the behaviour of verbs under passivisation (using my judgements, or your own, or both)
to attempt to decide between possible alternative
interpretations.

There is a considerable residue of verbs which
have neither affected object nor an idiomatic link
with their preposition, but which still allow
passivisation. Some examples:
40. a. The sea here can safely be paddled in by
toddlers
b. The sands are occasionally parked on by
incautious drivers
c. Was this the phone booth phoned from by
the kidnappers?
d. The man on the ledge was pleaded with to
come down
e. Even the bed was peered under by his
suspicious mother-in-law
f. Help has been phoned for
There are also differences between prepositions:
from is very short both on passivisable verbs and
on idiomatic or affected-object constructions.
Under is short on the latter, but passive is still
possible more often. For appears to have a marked
affinity for idiomatic linkage. However, I have no
very precise ideas about what to do with the rest of
this data. Have you?
There is one more distinction, related fairly
closely to the distinction of idiomatic and non-
idiomatic connection, which appears to have some
relevance to passivisability. This is the distinction which is sometimes made between 'actants' and
'circonstants' (using French labels in the absence
of standard English labels). An **actant** is a NP
which forms part of the 'core' of participants in
the action (state, process, etc.) conveyed by a
verb. E.g. given a verb like steal, we know that it
will be associated with an Agent (stealer), Patient
(thing stolen) and a Loser (person robbed), whether
these things are expressed or not. These are its
actants. But there will also be other circumstances
surrounding the robbery - its location, time, purpose, person benefiting, etc. These are circonstants, not actants, because they are characterist-

ic of all actions, not just stealing, and so do not form part of the characteristic environment of stealing. Actants are more likely to be passivisable than circonstants; e.g. given a verb like pounce, it can be used with a preposition to convey an actant - the person/thing which is the target of the pouncing. However, it can also be used without an expressed target, but with a location specified with the same preposition. It is only in the former use that the passive is natural:

41. a. The sheep was pounced on by the wolf
    b. ?*The railway platform was pounced on by the assassins

(NB, (41b) is fine in the unlikely event that the assassins did something to the railway platform; but as the passive of a sentence where the railway platform is the scene of the assassins' pouncing, it is virtually uninterpretable.)

READING - CHAPTER 4

The best discussion of this construction is by Dwight Bolinger 'Transitivity and spatiality' in Linguistics at the Crossroads (ed. Makkai, Makkai & Heilmann), Padova 1977. Cf. also Bolinger's book Meaning and Form Longman 1978. A. Davison 'Peculiar passives', Language 56: 42-66, 1980, covers English and many other languages in relation to this type of construction, while the notion of 'affected object' is discussed in S. Anderson 'Comments on the paper by Wasow' in Formal Syntax (ed. A. Akmajian, P. Culicover & T. Wasow) New York: Academic Press, 1979. (This article is difficult because of its specific theoretical orientation, although what it discusses is quite straightforward; the Wasow paper is relevant for our next chapter.) The distinction of 'actants' and 'circonstants' is made in L. Tesnière Eléments de syntaxe structurale, Paris: Klincksieck, 1959, and has been much taken up and developed since then.

Chapter Five

PASSIVE PARTICIPLES

In a sentence such as (1), is the participle <u>hurt</u> to be considered an adjective or a verb? And whichever way this question is answered, does the same hold true for all other passive participles?

    1. John was hurt by her response

These are innocent-sounding questions: indeed, it would not be difficult to dismiss them as being somewhat scholastic. There is currently considerable debate on this topic within transformational grammar (or rather, post-transformational grammar), but the questions which are at issue there are rather narrowly theoretical and depend on assumptions which, in spite of being taken for granted in most such research, are scarcely argued for at all. However, a detailed discussion of this issue raises a host of substantive problems as well, and casts some doubt on the whole notion of there being clear distinctions between grammatical categories.

    The criteria by which we can distinguish adjectives from verbs fall into two types: firstly we can distinguish **lexical** categories by the range of contexts in which they occur - e.g. verbs are the only elements which can form a predicate (VP) on their own in English. But criteria of this sort do not help us with passive participles: we know that they are **related** to verbs - what we want to know is whether they are simply one **form** which verbs can take, or whether they are separate words related to verbs by processes of derivation. Fortunately the second set of criteria **can** be used to make such a distinction; if passive participles are adjectives, we should expect them to have the features in (2), while if they are verbs we expect them to lack those features, but possibly to have the features in (3):

    2. a. Adjectives have comparative and super-
            lative forms

      b. Adjectives can be modified by <u>very</u>, <u>rather</u>, etc.

      c. Adjectives occur both after a form of <u>be</u> and before a noun within the noun phrase

      d. Adjectives occur as the complement of verbs such as <u>prove</u>, <u>seem</u>, <u>become</u>, <u>feel</u>

      e. Adjectives often have a negative form in <u>un-</u>

      f. Adjectives may be turned into adverbs by the addition of <u>-ly</u>

      g. Adjectives may often be turned into nouns by the addition of <u>-ness</u> or an equivalent suffix

      h. Adjectives are conjoinable with other adjectives

3. a. Verbs may be modified by <u>much</u> rather than <u>very</u>

      b. Verbs occur in the context NP <u>saw/heard/had</u> NP ___

      c. Verbs modifying nouns occur after the noun

To anticipate, it turns out that some participles are very like adjectives, while others are very like verbs. I exemplify a <u>bona fide</u> adjective (4), an adjective-like participle (5) and a verb-like participle (6):

4. a. John is happier, but Mary is happiest
    b. John is very happy
    c. He is a very happy man
    d. He seems happy enough to me
    e. He became unhappy when she died
    f. He smiled happily
    g. Happiness is what he aims for
    h. He was both rich and happy
    i. *We are all much happy
    j. *We heard him happy
    k. *The man happy was John

5. a. John is tireder than Mary
    b. He is very tired
    c. He is a tired little boy
    d. He felt tired
    e. ??He remains untired
    f. He was overcome by tiredness
    g. ?He slumped down tiredly
    h. Are you tired and weary?
    i. *I was much tired
    j. *I saw him tired
    k. *The man tired had been running

6. a. **John is hitter than Mary
    b. *John was very hit
    c. *It was a hit target
    d. *The target seems hit
    e. ?The target remained unhit

     f. *The hitness of the target is quite low
     g. *He collapsed hitly
     h. *He was ill and hit
     i. ?The target was much hit
     j. I saw it hit
     k. The target hit is the one on the left

There are some slight anomalies here, which we shall consider briefly soon. On the whole, however, the pattern is a clear one; if all participles fitted this pattern it would be perfectly satisfactory to say that some participles are adjectives, and some are verbs, and leave it at that. As you might have guessed, however, things are not that simple. There are two problems: different participles behave quite differently with respect to these criteria; and different native speakers of English behave quite differently in their judgements.

There is a further complicating factor which we can consider briefly first. That is that the criteria of (2) do not apply equally to all adjectives (cf. *unred, *bluely, *ruralness, *very absolute, etc.) The strategy we shall have to adopt is therefore a rather roundabout one. We first need to ask about the subset of adjectives to which each criterion applies - e.g. very might be said to modify all **gradable** adjectives. We can then eliminate some or all participles on the grounds that - even if they were real adjectives - they would not occur in this subset of adjectives. E.g. we have to exclude all participles which are not gradable. We might also expect problems of definition here; what does it mean for a participle to be gradable? Life is hard.

5.2. HOW MESSY IS THE DATA?

The comparative construction has some curious complications when used with participles. We can distinguish its normal use from a rather divergent use which applies to virtually all participles, and to noun phrases as well:
    7. a. He is more sinning than sinned against
       b. He is more a social worker than a managing
          director
What is at issue in this construction is not degree of a property, but rather the appropriateness of one designation as opposed to another in relation to the subject NP. The 'normal' comparative construction compares the intensity of a quality in two different subjects. With normal adjectives there is a distinc-

tion to be made on more or less purely phonological
grounds between the use of the suffix -er and the
analytic form more; the suffix occurs with monosyllabic and disyllabic adjectives, while the analytic form can be used with two or more syllables.
The construction in (7), by contrast, always
involves the form more. A very few participles
appear to allow the suffixal form (cf. (5a)), but on
the whole those participles which are compatible
with the comparative allow only the analytic form,
even if they are monosyllabic:

    8. a. My coat is more worn than yours
       b. *My coat is worner than yours
    9. a. His mother was more vexed than his father
       b. *His mother was vexeder than his father

These complications apart, the distribution of the
comparative form with participles appears to be much
the same as that of very, although I find minor
differences of acceptability in some cases:

    10. a. Our organisation is more unified than it
          was
      b.??Our organisation is very unified

An even clearer case where comparative is possible
but very is not comes from a letter to a newspaper:

    11. Does this mean that child abuse has become
      more tolerated when perpetrated against young
      girls than young boys?

On the whole, however, those participles which do
not admit one of these forms do not admit the other
either, and the same is true mutatis mutandis for
those which do occur in these forms.

    The use of participles as prenominal modifiers
is one of the most complex of these criteria. Virtually all participles occur as postnominal modifiers,
and the difference between forms such as the stolen
jewels and the jewels stolen has been the subject of
much discussion (most illuminatingly, by Bolinger).
Very roughly, the distinction corresponds to the
difference between specifying an inherent quality of
the noun (with a prenominal modifier) and identify-
ing the noun with reference to a particular event
(with a postnominal modifier). Someone might be
handling stolen jewels without any knowledge of the
particular robbery or robberies at which they were
stolen, but stolen jewels have the inherent property
that they are dangerous to handle. By contrast the
jewels stolen must refer to some particular robbery
or robberies. It seems fairly apparent that if a
'characteristic' reading cannot be obtained with a
participle, it will not occur in prenominal position. This is no doubt why the prenominal use of

participles is so much more acceptable when they are
modified by a manner adverbial of some kind:

    12. a. *The resolved problem had always troubled
           him
       b. The successfully resolved problem had
          always troubled him
    13. a. *Everyone was angry about the retracted
          offer
       b. Everyone was angry about the suddenly
          retracted offer.

So once again, as with the comparative form, it can
be seen that participles show behaviour which is
somewhat reminiscent of adjective behaviour, but not
quite the same; there are no adjectives (are there?)
which occur in prenominal position only when they
are adverbially modified.

I shall return to the problem of <u>seem</u>, <u>prove</u>,
<u>become</u>, etc. in the next section; although there are
specific differences between each of these verbs,
any adjective ought to be able to co-occur with at
least one of them, and therefore as a group they are
a fairly reliable criterion of adjectivehood.

<u>Un-</u> is different again; although it is often
cited as a criterion of adjectival status, it in
fact applies to a rather small subclass of adjectives, while it is extremely regular with participles. In fact, of the few participles which it does
not occur with, several are the most adjective-like
of the participles (cf. *<u>unupset</u>, *<u>unpleased</u>).
Incidentally, there is no doubt that the derived
form (with <u>un-</u>) is very adjective-like; what is at
issue is the form from which it is derived. An
apparent exception illustrates rather the shock
value inherent in use of <u>un-</u>participles in a non-
adjectival function:

    14. [I] simply record the fact that I was not
       unemployed in my profession by the late John
       Jacob Astor (H. Melville 'Bartleby')

There is certainly something strange about claiming
that participles are adjectives on the basis of a
criterion which applies with much greater regularity
to participles than it does to adjectives. The
distribution of <u>un-</u> clearly needs to be looked at in
a lot more detail.

The suffixes -<u>ness</u> and -<u>ly</u> can be taken
together, as they are both rather restricted in
their occurrence with participles. With true adjectives, however, they are both quite productive, -<u>ly</u>
more so than -<u>ness</u>, which is only one of a number of
ways of deriving nouns from adjectives (cf. <u>able</u> -
<u>ability</u>, for instance), although it is the most

productive by far. There is one major difference
between these two forms: -ness is semantically
rather neutral, but -ly can be paraphrased as 'in a
___manner'. It is therefore hardly plausible to
claim that there is a semantic motivation behind the
lack of a noun such as *understoodness, but the lack
of an adverb *understoodly follows quite straight-
forwardly from the semantic deviance of a phrase
such as *in an understood manner.

The criterion that elements of the same category can be conjoined is not reliable, but can be a
useful additional criterion. (15) is a case where it
is unreliable:

15. Your argument is obscure and of little
relevance

However, the more adjective-like participles do
conjoin quite freely with true adjectives (16),
while those which are less adjective-like may not,
even with a certain amount of plausible context:

16. a. Poor John was anxious and worried
b. His pleased and happy smile said
everything

17. a. *We keep that watch in the safe because
it is both sold and valuable
b. *The sewn and bright red patches on his
jeans shocked everyone

There is a rather fine line to be drawn, of course,
between simple conjunction and the addition of
afterthoughts, which can look like conjoined
elements but be quite acceptable even where the
normal coordinate form would not be:

18. I'm afraid that watch is rather too
expensive ... and sold anyway

The use of much with past participles allows
two interpretations. On one, which is also possible
with the corresponding finite form of the verb, it
indicates a high degree of some state:

19. a. I much appreciate your advice
b. Your advice is much appreciated

In the other interpretation it refers to multiple
occurrences of the same action; much stolen jewels
are jewels which have been stolen many times. It is
this latter interpretation which occurs most generally.

Finally, the other criterion for verbhood
applies exclusively to action verbs, and may involve
either the passive participle, or the basic form of
the verb, or the -ing participle. Adjectives do not
occur in this construction.

20. a. I saw the bomb exploded
b. Everybody heard him told off

        c. The teacher had him flogged
 21. a. I saw the bomb explode
     b. Everybody heard him being told off
     c. *The teacher had him happy
Table 5.1. shows these features as they apply to a
range of participles.
     It can be seen from the table that the situat-
ion is really quite messy. (Note that the table
makes no pretensions to being representative, or to
covering the full range of variability in the
behaviour of participles.) Modification by <u>very</u> or
<u>more</u>, and the addition of -<u>ly</u> or -<u>ness</u>, are the most
restricted possibilities in the table, but they do
not coincide with each other, nor are they wholly
included in the possibilities permitted by less
restrictive criteria. <u>Un-</u> is the only one of the
adjective criteria which applies to a wide range of
participles, but we have already seen that there is
reason to doubt that <u>un-</u> is in any simple sense an
adjectival criterion.

EXERCISE 1

Go through the data in the table in rather more
detail, trying to account for judgements where possible with semantic criteria or other constraints on
the occurrence of these forms. Many of the judgements on the table will come apart with a little
more probing - e.g. <u>recognise</u> might plausibly be
analysed as two different verbs, each with different
behaviour with respect to these criteria. On the
basis of this detailed analysis of the table (and of
other data if you can bring yourself to add further
to it), is it possible to make a distinction between
those participles which are adjectives and those
which are not? Or is there any other distinction
which seems to emerge?

5.3. HOW RELIABLE ARE INTUITIVE JUDGEMENTS?

You may disagree with some of the judgements in
Table 5.1. Most people do disagree with other
people's intuitive judgements in at least some
instances, unless the nature of the data is exceedingly obvious. This is to be distinguished from
differences between genuine dialects, which can be
localised and discussed with reference to the overall grammatical system of a particular dialect.

Passive participles

Table 5.1. Syntactic behaviour of some participles

	1	2	3		4	5	6	7	8	9	10
agreed	−	−	+	sum	+	?	−	−	+	−	−
allowed	−	−	−		−	−	−	−	−	−	−
analysed	−	−	−		−	+	−	−	−	+	+
appreciated	−	−	−		+	+	?	?	?	+	−
confiscated	−	−	−		−	+	−	−	−	+	+
contradicted	−	−	−		−	+	−	−	−	+	−
cut	−	−	+	flowers	−	+	−	−	−	?	+
disgusted	+	?	+	look	+	−	+	+	+	−	−
finished	−	−	+	product	+	+	−	−	+	?	+
grown	−	−	−	(11)	−	+	−	−	?	+	+
hated	+	−	+	tyrant	+	−	−	−	?	+	−
hit	−	−	−		−	+	−	−	−	+	+
joined	−	−	+	ends	?	+	−	−	−	−	?
lost	−	−	−		+	−	−	−	−	?	−
polluted	+	+	+		+	+	−	+	+	−	?
postponed	−	−	−		−	+	−	−	−	+	+
prevented	−	−	−		−	−	−	−	−	−	+
recognised	?	−	?	authority	+	+	−	−	+	−	+
recommended	−	−	+	text	−	?	−	−	−	+	+
resolved	−	−	−		+	+	−	−	?	?	+
seen	−	−	−		−	+	−	−	−	+	−
sewn	−	−	−		−	+	−	−	−	+	+
sold	−	−	−		−	+	−	−	−	?	+
swallowed	−	−	−		?	+	−	−	−	+	+
understood	−	−	?	subject	+	−	−	−	−	−	−
undergone	−	−	−		−	−	−	−	−	?	−
watched	−	−	??	pot	−	+	−	−	−	+	+

1. has a comparative form
2. may be modified by very
3. occurs prenominally (? indicates heavily restricted use: the noun mentioned is a typical modified noun for that participle). NB Virtually all participles occur prenominally when they are themselves adverbially modified.
4. occurs as complement of seem, etc.
5. takes the prefix un-
6. takes the suffix - ly
7. takes the suffix - ness
8. conjoins with normal adjectives
9. may be modified by much
10. occurs as second complement of see, etc.
11. grown man is not passive

E.g. if you disagree with my intuitive judgement on
(12a) above, no reliable conclusions can be drawn
from that about where you come from. If, however,
you disagree with my judgement on (22), it is likely
that you are American:
    22. *I want you should come and see me
(NB not all Americans accept sentences like (22)) It
has occasionally been suggested that the existence
of such 'non-localised' differences relates to areas
where the data available to language learners is
simply insufficient for them to induce a unique
rule. It would still be to determine, even then, how
much order there was in this variation.
    I presented a class of linguistics students
with the questionnaire of Table 5.2 before broaching
the topic of past participles with them. The results
for <u>seem</u> are tabulated in Table 5.3 (courtesy of
Richard Evered). (1)-(13) along the top row represent the individual respondents to the questionnaire. Even a fairly superficial glance at the
tables shows that there was a considerable variety
of responses, disagreement being commoner than
agreement. Any attempt to read some neat hierarch-
ical order into the results seems doomed to failure.
    Of course, those who are sophisticated in the
design of experiments will see that this one was
rather badly designed. One might ask: what was the
basis for selecting the verbs? Is there any effect
on the responses conditioned by the order in which
the verbs and contexts were presented? Is the scale
of gradations appropriate? Were the instructions
clear? (But remember that these were linguistics
students.) Should the subjects have been linguists?
And so on. The responses to many of these questions
are quite unclear; it has been found that the
intuitions given by linguists are often fairly
consistently different from those given by non-
linguists. But does this indicate that linguists
have a fundamentally different type of linguistic
intuitions, or could it just be that linguists have
rather more training at filtering out factors related to the naturalness of particular sentences in
particular contexts, and at inventing far-fetched
contexts where particular sentences would be the
natural thing to say?
    We could try various techniques of approaching
these data: e.g. if we accept the data of Table 5.3
as reliable data for the moment, we could try the
method of **implicational scaling.** In the ideal cases,
two verbs will participate on an implicational scale
when the judgements on one verb are positive only

Table 5.2.   Description of English. Questionnaire
_____

Put a judgement (tick, cross, or question mark)
against each of the passive participles in each
sentence frame.

                    That seems__ It became__ It proved __

agreed
allowed
analysed
appreciated
confiscated
contradicted
cut
finished
grown
hated
hit
joined
lost
polluted
postponed
prevented
recognised
recommended
resolved
seen
sewn
sold
swallowed
understood
undergone
watched
_____

when those on another verb are positive, but not
vice versa. I.e. all speakers accept sentences such
as (23), only some speakers accept sentences such as
(22), and no speakers (well, fewer, at least) accept
sentences such as (24):
    23. I want to go
    24. *I want Mary has finished
These judgements therefore form an implicational
scale, as the acceptability of (22) implies the
acceptability of (23), but not vice versa. When more
normal sets of intuitions are compared, it is often
possible to compile imperfect implicational scales,

Passive participles

Table 5.3. Results of the questionnaire for the frame 'That seems ___

		1	2	3	4	5	6	7	8	9	10	11	12	13	+	−	?
a.	agreed	+	+	+	+	−	+	+	+	+	+	+	+	+	12	1	0
b.	allowed	?	+	?	+	+	?	−	?	+	+	−	+	+	7	2	4
c.	analysed	−	+	+	?	−	−	−	−	?	+	+	+	+	6	5	2
d.	appreciated	?	+	+	?	+	+	+	−	+	?	+	−	+	8	2	3
e.	confiscated	−	+	−	?	−	−	−	−	−	−	−	−	−	1	11	1
f.	contradicted	−	+	−	?	+	+	−	+	+	+	−	+	+	8	4	1
g.	cut	−	+	−	?	−	+	−	?	−	+	+	−	+	5	6	2
h.	finished	+	+	+	+	+	+	−	+	+	+	+	+	+	12	1	0
i.	grown	−	+	−	−	−	?	−	−	−	+	+	−	?	3	8	2
j.	hated	?	+	−	?	+	+	−	−	−	?	−	−	+	4	6	3
k.	hit	−	+	−	−	−	−	−	−	−	?	−	−	+	2	10	1
l.	joined	−	+	?	?	+	+	−	+	?	+	+	+	+	8	2	3
m.	lost	+	+	−	+	+	+	−	+	+	+	+	+	+	11	2	0
n.	polluted	+	+	+	+	+	+	−	+	+	+	+	+	+	12	1	0
o.	postponed	−	+	−	?	−	−	−	−	?	+	−	−	?	2	8	3
p.	prevented	−	+	?	−	−	−	−	+	?	−	−	−	+	3	8	2
q.	recognised	+	?	+	+	−	+	+	+	+	+	−	+	+	10	2	1
r.	recommended	−	+	+	+	−	+	−	?	?	−	+	+	?	6	4	3
s.	resolved	+	+	+	+	+	+	+	+	+	+	+	+	+	13	0	0
t.	seen	−	?	−	?	−	−	−	−	−	−	−	−	?	0	10	3
u.	sewn	−	+	−	+	+	−	−	?	−	+	+	−	+	6	6	1
v.	sold	−	+	?	?	−	+	−	+	−	+	+	−	+	6	5	2
w.	swallowed	−	+	−	?	−	+	−	−	−	+	+	?	+	5	6	2
x.	understood	+	+	+	+	+	+	+	+	+	+	+	+	+	13	0	0
y.	undergone	−	?	−	−	−	−	−	−	−	−	−	−	−	0	12	1
z.	watched	−	+	?	−	+	−	−	−	−	+	−	−	?	3	8	2
	+	7	23	9	10	12	15	5	11	10	18	15	12	19			
	−	16	0	12	5	14	9	21	11	11	5	11	13	2			
	?	3	3	5	11	0	2	0	4	5	3	0	1	5			

The right-hand columns give the number of speakers giving judgements for each verb, while the bottom rows give the number of verbs for which each speaker gave judgements.

where a few speakers 'misbehave'. As with simple addition of judgements, the final stage of this analysis is then to compare the scale with semantic (or other) features of the participles, to see if there is any correlation. However, the table is not encouraging about this possibility either: speaker 11, for instance, allows the evenly divided <u>sold</u>, but excludes the popular <u>recognised</u>; speaker 2 totally rejects nothing, and is the only one fully to accept <u>confiscated</u>: but also casts doubt on <u>recognised</u>.

It would be nice if textual data could be found to throw light on the use of such constructions. But if speakers genuinely differ in using these constructions, we would need data on sociolinguistic variation in their use. Imagine what we would need:

A. sentences containing <u>seem</u>: assume (probably conservatively) that English texts would contain one occurrence of <u>seem</u> for every thousand simple sentences.

B. cases where the complement of <u>seem</u> is a passive participle: it would probably also be generous to assume that one in a thousand of the sentences of A would fit this condition.

C. we would need a number of speakers (say ten) and a good number of tokens of the relevant sentence type for each of them (100?).

So we filter one thousand million (!) clauses of English text: it is still not certain that there would be sufficient data to distinguish interesting cases. Perhaps all occurring types would involve participles like <u>agreed</u>, <u>understood</u>, <u>tired</u>, etc. where there is little disagreement. We would be as far as ever from an understanding of which participles may occur with <u>seem</u>. It is fairly safe to conclude that 'objective' methods in the study of sociolinguistic variation, whatever their merits in general, are at best only capable of application to a small subset of syntactic problems.

There are, of course, other ways in which we could attempt to organise the data. Naturally it would be preferable to conduct more sophisticated types of tests for intuitions before doing this. However, it seems that we need to reconcile ourselves to the possibility that certain phenomena simply yield no highly recognisable pattern when the judgements of different speakers are sampled. The implications of this state of affairs for language teaching, for instance, should be obvious. It is perhaps not too much to be wondered at that there should be such a situation, that there should be limits on what we can hope to find out about. It may be that prototype semantics applies to linguistic units too, that grammatical regularities should be statable in terms of the most typical members of a category, and that they should only be extended piecemeal over less central members. How such a situation might correspond to real linguistic behaviour in detail is of course another question.

READING - CHAPTER 5

Three articles on the adjectival status of passive participles: R. Freidin 'On the analysis of passive' Language 51 (1975), J. Bresnan 'Towards a realistic approach to grammar' in J. Bresnan, M. Halle & G. Miller (eds) Linguistic Theory and Psychological Reality Cambridge, Mass.: MIT, T. Wasow 'Transformations and the lexicon' in P. Culicover et al. Formal Syntax (Academic Press). The last two of these are subjected to a critique in D. Kilby 'On lexical approaches to the passive' University of Essex Dept. of Lang. & Ling. Occasional Papers 25.
   For adjective position, see D. Bolinger 'Adjectives in English: attribution or predication?' Lingua 18 (1967). There is a whole literature growing on what is called 'variation theory'; the Chambers and Trudgill work mentioned in the introduction provides the basic ideas and bibliography. On reliability of intuitions, several useful articles appear in C. J. Fillmore, D. Kempler and W. S-Y. Wang (eds) Individual Differences in Language Ability and Language Behaviour, New York: Academic Press, 1979.

Chapter Six

PHRASAL VERBS

In chapter 4 I have already briefly considered the
nature of phrasal verbs, in distinguishing them from
prepositional verbs. To recap, there are sentences
which contain a prepositional verb construction
(1a), others with a phrasal verb construction (1b)
and yet others are ambiguous (1c):
    1. a. Jack ran down the hill
       b. Jill ran down her business activities
       c. Jack and Jill ran down the factory
Phrasal verbs can appropriately be analysed with a
structure as in (2), while prepositional verbs have
a structure as in (3):

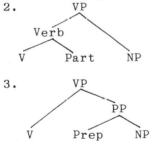

2.

3.

(NB the choice of <u>Verb</u> as a node label has no significance; it could equally well be <u>verb group</u>, or
an arbitrary symbol such as X.)
    There is a certain amount of redundancy in the
labelling here: the constituent structure would be
sufficient to distinguish phrasal and prepositional
verbs, even if particles were 'really' prepositions,
as has often been proposed. But the class of particles and the class of prepositions, though they
overlap quite considerably, are not identical: <u>back</u>
is syntactically a particle, but can never be used
prepositionally, while certain prepositions such as

<u>at</u>, <u>for</u>, <u>from</u>, <u>of</u>, <u>to</u> (if we exclude marginal expressions like 'shut the door to') and <u>with</u> are never used in phrasal verb constructions. Just to avoid confusion, I also ought to mention that the use of the term 'particle' in connection with phrasal verbs is to be kept quite distinct from the general linguistic use of 'particle' to mean any small and relatively insignificant word.

The criteria for distinguishing particles from prepositions have already been dealt with in chapter four. There is a further set of criteria by which particles can be distinguished from adverbs, as in (4):

4. a. He pushed the window up
   b. He pushed the window upwards

Adverbs are (although in varying degrees) significantly less happy before a simple definite noun phrase than particles are:

5. a. He pushed up the window
   b. ?He pushed upwards the window
   c. *He pushed awkwardly the window

Adverbs may often be preposed to the beginning of the sentence, while particles cannot, unless the whole syntax of the sentence is being altered:

6. a. ??Up he pushed the window
   b. ?Upwards he pushed the window
   c. Awkwardly he pushed the window
   d. Up went the window

Clefts and pseudo-clefts are much more readily formed with adverbs than with particles:

7. a. It was upwards that he pushed the window
   b. *It was up that he pushed the window
8. a. ??Where he pushed the window was up
   b. Where he pushed the window was upwards

Finally, and perhaps most reliably, particles may follow a participial form of the verb as a prenominal modifier (e.g. <u>a</u> <u>pulled-down</u> <u>blind</u>, <u>washed-up</u> <u>dishes</u>), a position which is quite excluded for adverbs (*<u>a</u> <u>pulled</u> <u>downwards</u> <u>blind</u>, *<u>thrown</u> <u>upwards</u> <u>boomerangs</u>). Unfortunately this criterion may not always be applicable, due to the sorts of complexities we looked at in chapter five.

If we agree that the criteria mentioned here are sufficient to distinguish a set of particles, and hence of phrasal verbs, we can articulate a set of problems which need to be answered before we can have anything approaching an adequate knowledge of the syntax and semantics of phrasal verbs. Here are some major questions:

9. Is there any definable set of verbs which occur with particles in general, or with particular

particles in particular?

10. Where do we draw the line between those phrasal verb combinations which are productive and semantically regular and those which are idiomatic and semantically opaque?

11. Do the different positions in which particles may occur - i.e. before and after the object NP - correlate with any other factor or set of factors?

Each of these questions provides enormous scope for developing extensive discussion; I shall restrict myself to a brief discussion of each of them, trying to bring out a few salient points about the various constructions, as well as posing more specific questions.

6.2. VERBS WHICH OCCUR WITH PARTICLES

There is not a lot of work done on this aspect of phrasal verb constructions; it is normally assumed that it is a question for the writers of dictionaries, and there are a few attempts (e.g. Fraser, and Cowie and Mackin) to write dictionaries of constructions such as these. Those linguists who have taken a heavily theoretical line towards this construction have tended to stay away from such messy questions. One of the few linguists to try to make sense of this (albeit with reference to only one particle in one of its uses) was Benjamin Lee Whorf, in a little-cited passage from his article 'A linguistic consideration of thinking in primitive communities' (appropriately enough). It is worth citing in full, as it is the only semantically-based discussion of such questions that I know:

> [A covert linguistic class] is a submerged, subtle and elusive meaning, corresponding to no actual word, yet shown by linguistic analysis to be functionally important in the grammar. For example, the English particle UP meaning 'completely, to a finish', as in 'break it up, cover it up, eat it up, twist it up, open it up' can be applied to any verb of one or two syllables initially accented, EXCEPTING verbs belonging to four special cryptotypes. One is the cryptotype of dispersion without boundary; hence one does not say 'spread it up, waste it up, spend it up, scatter it up, drain it up or filter it up'. Another is the cryptotype of oscillation without agitation of parts; we don't say 'rock up a cradle, wave up a flag, wiggle up

a finger, nod up one's head', etc. The third is
the cryptotype of nondurative impact which also
includes psychological reaction: kill, fight,
etc., hence we don't say 'whack it up, tap it
up, stab it up, slam it up, wrestle him up, hate
him up'. The fourth is the verbs of directed
motion, move, lift, pull, push, put, etc., with
which UP has the directional sense 'upward', or
derived senses, even though this sense may be
contradicted by the verb and hence produce an
effect of absurdity, as in 'drip it up'. Outside
this set of cryptotypes, UP may be freely used
with transitives in the completive-intensive
sense. (B. L. Whorf Language, Thought and
Reality MIT Press, 1956, pp70-71.)

It is easy to laugh at Whorf's semantic classification; it is less easy, though possible, to find
counterexamples to it. The condition about monosyllabic and disyllabic initially-accented words is
essentially an etymological one: Germanic and
assimilated Romance vocabulary fits this classification; later loans from Romance which are less well
assimilated do not occur with particles at all on
the whole. This is very noticeable in a dictionary
such as that of Cowie and Mackin which includes
prepositional verbs; verbs with Romance prefixes
(con-, de-, ex-, etc.) hardly ever occur in phrasal
verb combinations.

There do appear to be further characteristic
features of phrasal verbs in general. For instance,
all phrasal verbs have resultative meaning of some
sort - i.e. they specify a state of affairs which
results from the action denoted by the verb. It
follows from this that the basic verbs from which
phrasal verb combinations are formed are nearly all
verbs of action; one apparent exception to this is
the verb think which can be the source for verbs
such as think up and think out - which are, however,
clearly resultative. In any case the classification
of think with respect to action is not entirely
clear.

It is also likely that some verbs will fail to
occur with any particles because there is simply no
combination of verb and particle meanings which
naturally makes sense. Thrive, for instance, which
might be put in Whorf's semantic class of dispersion
without boundary, is not apparently the sort of verb
which would naturally lend itself to a resultative
meaning, i.e. there is no natural result of thriv-
ing. But there are also verbs which have an entirely

determinate result which do not allow the formation
of phrasal verbs with the exhaustive meaning of <u>up</u> -
e.g. <u>wreck</u>, <u>wound</u> and <u>hurt</u>. Some light can be cast
on such cases by considering the meanings attached
to verbs which <u>do</u> form phrasal combinations of this
sort. There seem to be two classes; one class
involves a simple verb which refers to an increase
in a scalar property - here the addition of <u>up</u>
suggests that the top end of the
scale is reached, e.g.

   12. He polished the silver

   13. He polished the silver up

(12) suggests the silver is more polished than
before, while (13) suggests that it is polished up
to a satisfactory shine. The other type involves an
action which is interpreted as applying only to
simple objects, and the addition of <u>up</u> makes it
applicable to more complex objects. The classic case
of this is <u>break</u>:

   14. He broke his arm (??his car)

   15. He broke up his car

These criteria suggest that with verbs like <u>wreck</u>
and <u>wound</u>, the former involves a determinate result
in relation to even the most complex of objects -
there is therefore nothing for the particle to add.
<u>Wound</u>, on the other hand, expresses an action which
can be repeated <u>ad</u> <u>lib</u>; but the only plausible
candidate for a natural endpoint for wounding is
something which cannot appropriately be termed
wounding - i.e. killing. On the basis of rather
speculative considerations such as these, we might
attempt to maintain the thesis that the possibility
of forming a phrasal verb with <u>up</u> in the exhaustive
meaning is purely a function of pragmatic factors.

6.3. REGULARITY AND IDIOMATICITY

There is a tendency for linguists to distinguish the
use of particles in a purely spatial sense from
other uses of particles, and to equate the two with
regular and idiomatic usage respectively. There is
certainly no doubt that the spatial use of particles
is regular; most verbs which specify movement in
space occur with the full range of particles, bar-
ring cases where the lexical meaning of the verb and
the meaning of the particle clash (as in ?<u>suck</u>
<u>round</u>). E.g. with only the verb <u>bring</u>, and only in
its spatial meanings, we get <u>bring</u> <u>up</u>, <u>bring</u> <u>out</u>,
<u>bring</u> <u>round</u>, <u>bring</u> <u>in</u>, etc. The meaning of these
combinations is also regular; the object which

undergoes the motion ends up in the position specified by the particle. If you bring something up,
it's up, etc. It is not surprising in view of this
that such combinations are commonly cited as **the**
regular type of phrasal verbs. But to say that all
other uses of phrasal verbs are idiomatic is a
misuse of the term. An idiom is a construction which
is both unproductive and which has an overall meaning quite different from what might be expected from
the meaning of the parts which make it up. It is
necessary, however, to distinguish idiomatic usage
from metaphorical usage (even though the two may be
historically related in one way or another). Look,
for instance, at the two meanings of
    16. He threw in the towel
Where it refers to a piece of cloth, the verb threw
and the particle in have their literal meanings, and
together yield the meaning of the whole. Where it
refers to giving up, however, this literal meaning
is absent; but the construction is metaphorical in
the sense that it can clearly be understood in
reference to a type of situation where a piece of
cloth actually is thrown into something (a ring) -
i.e. it is taking the features of one situation and
transferring their significance to another situation. But compare it with another usage of throw in:
    17. If you pay cash, I'll throw in a car radio
              as well
Here there is no question of an action of throwing
or of physical interiority; it may be that such
expressions could be understood with reference to
some historical circumstances where 'genuine' throwing occurred in such transactions, but there is
little doubt that in synchronic terms throw in is
merely a casual way of saying 'include', and is
therefore (to at least some degree) idiomatic.
    There are certainly many phrasal verb combi-
nations which strike us intuitively as being
idiomatic - i.e. the verb's meaning and the meaning
of the particle do not simply combine to make up the
meaning of the combination. Give in or do in are
examples of this type. However, the notion of idiomaticity should not be entirely dependent on our
intuitions; it is often possible to find through
linguistic analysis that there **is** a regular meaning
involved in such combinations - Whorf's analysis of
the meaning of up as 'completely' is just one such
example. A classic case of idiom such as 'kick the
bucket' (= 'die') is not just idiomatic because we
feel that it is, but because no other use of kick,
the or bucket can be analysed as having a meaning

which corresponds in part to the meaning of die. If kick were more widely used in its sense of 'quit' (as in kick the habit), and if the bucket was a way of referring to life (putting all your eggs in one bucket, perhaps), then the phrase would **not** be idiomatic - or at least not in the same degree. Once again, the demonstration that something is not totally idiomatic is simply a matter of providing sufficient data for a variety of regularities to emerge. A further important point which follows from this discussion is that idiomaticity is a **scalar** property - from total regularity to total absence of semantic motivation.

As a pilot study, I shall consider some uses of the particles up and down; Table 6.1 is a reference list of the first hundred verbs which combine with up to make phrasal verbs in Cowie and Mackin's dictionary, and the 40 verbs which combine with down in the same part of the dictionary.

One use of up which I have already mentioned is its use as a spatial particle, indicating that the action involves motion from a lower point to a higher point. E.g. bob up, bring up (in one sense), buoy up, chuck up, etc. all fit this characterisation to a greater or lesser degree. There is a further spatial use of the particle up referring to the closeness of the target position to some object, as in (18):

18. He went up to the statue and looked at the inscription

This is exemplified by another use of bring up, and by come up, creep up, etc. It is not entirely clear to me what the restrictions are on this use of up, but in principle both of these uses are capable of occurring with any verb involving motion in space.

The use referred to by Whorf is the completive use of up: here the verb used without up denotes an action, and the particle sets the natural limit on the action, showing that the state of affairs in which the action normally concludes has been achieved, cf:

19. a. He wiped the table
    b. He wiped the table up

E.g. from our list add up, beat up, blow up, board up, etc. It should be clear that if there is no natural end to the process denoted by the verb, then that verb is unlikely to occur in this use. One of the clearest ways of exemplifying this is through verbs which are simple process words when they are used intransitively, but have a natural conclusion (in Comrie's terms, they are **telic**) when they are

Table 6.1   Verbs combining with <u>up</u> and <u>down</u> to make phrasal verbs.

up			down
act	chain	curl	back
add	chalk	cut	bear
back	chase	dam	beat
bank	chat	dig	bed
bear	check	dish	blow
beat	cheer	do	bog
blow	choke	doll	boil
board	chop	double	bolt
bob	chuck	drag	break
boil	churn	draw	bring
bolster	clam	dream	brush
bone	clean	dredge	buckle
book	clear	dress	burn
botch	clog	drink	call
bottle	close	drum	calm
box	clutter	dry	cast
break	cock	earth	chop
brew	coil	ease	clamp
bring	come	eat	clean
brush	conjure	end	climb
bubble	connect	even	close
buck	cook	face	come
bugger	coop	fatten	cool
build	cork	fetch	copy
bump	cough	fill	count
bung	count	finish	crack
buoy	couple	fit	cut
burn	cover	fix	damp
bust	crack	flare	die
butter	crank	fold	do
buy	creep		doss
call	crisp		draw
carve	crop		dress
cast	crumple		drink
catch	crush		dust
			ease
			fall
			fight
			flag
			flop

used transitively:
    20. a. When he was young, John read all the time
       b. *When he was young, John read up all the
           time
    21. a. John read a whole library of books last
          year
       b. John read up a whole library of books
However, this appears to be essentially a pragmatic
restriction on the possibility of forming a phrasal
verb - a particle adding a meaning of 'completion'
cannot be used in a context where the notion of
completion cannot naturally be interpreted. It seems
rather odd to claim that the use of up in this sense
is other than productive, given that the major
restrictions on its use appear to be etymological
(unassimilated Romance doesn't work with it) and
pragmatic (verbs without a natural end point don't
work with it).

    Down so far correlates only with the first
spatial use of up, indicating the reverse direction.
It does not correlate with the second spatial use of
up: if you go up to somebody and then distance
yourself, you are not going down from them. Similarly, down has no parallel or opposite meaning to the
exhaustive use of up; indeed it is far from simple
to think of what such an opposite meaning might be.
However, there is another use of both up and down
which appears to involve a regular semantic opposition between them. Consider the following sentences:
    22. Tesco opened up a store in Bradford and
        closed one down in Bingley
    23. Someone let his tyres down, so he pumped
        them up again
    24. Do you want me to thicken this soup up, or
        thin it down?
    25. He wasn't sure whether to stoke the fire up
        or damp it down
I would contend that up is the 'active' member in
these sentences, while down is the inactive one.
This is probably obvious for all of these sentences
except (24): this pair clearly relates to the adjectives thick and thin. It is well known within
English grammar that adjectives in such antonymous
pairs are not of entirely equal status; one of them
is 'unmarked', in the sense that it is used in
scalar questions (such as (26)) unless there is a
strong presupposition that the marked member is
valid:
    26. a. How thick is that soup?
       b. How thin is that soup?
As a neutral question (26a) would be used, while

(26b) would on the whole only be used when it was clear that the soup was going to be pretty thin, the question perhaps being asked to see if the soup is edible (or potable). The same is true of the derivation of nouns from adjectives: if I talk about the thickness of the soup, I am not necessarily suggesting that the soup is thick, whereas to talk of the thinness of the soup carries with it the clear suggestion that the soup is thin. The same is true of many antonymous adjectival pairs, e.g.:

sharp - blunt fat - thin wide - narrow
rough - smooth clean - dirty open - closed
alive - dead hot - cold

Although not all of these have a phrasal verb corresponding to them (e.g. *blunt down), those that do form phrasal verbs tend rather strongly to conform to the up-down pairing of unmarkedness-markedness. The label 'idiomatic' would therefore seem to be rather inappropriate for this class of phrasal verbs too. From the up column of Table 6.1 we have bear up, boil up (?could be exhaustive reading too), bolster up (likewise), brew up, bring up (educationally), etc. From the down list, back down, bog down, break down, burn down, cast down, calm down, etc.

These subclasses of up and down use do cover most of the uses of the verbs in Table 6.1, although by no means all. By implication the 'residue' is either idiomatic/metaphorical or else to be subsumed under some other generalisation. Among the former, we would presumably include clean up in the sense 'make a lot of money', or dry up in the sense 'stop talking suddenly'. A possible further generalisation might relate up to the 'top' end of evaluative scales - cf. blow up 'praise excessively', build up 'speak of glowingly', butter up 'flatter', crack up, do up, doll up, dress up, etc. One classificatory problem here is that there is some considerable overlap between classes. However this is only a problem if we insist that there be disjoint subclasses: in fact it may turn out to be a useful entry into the question of how these classes developed. For instance, it is not unreasonable to class in the completive use of up such expressions as connect up (the electricity), fill up (the tank), fix up (some shelves), brew up (some tea), etc. But these could also have the 'active' interpretation: there is no contradiction about such double appropriateness.

It may be, therefore, that there are further subregularities within the up-down data, and I suspect that similar types of result could be obtained with other particles (in, out, etc.). Note that apparently minimal pairs will often involve quite different interpretations (chop up and chop down being an example which comes readily to mind, cf. also close up/down, drink up/down). One final point in this section; there are indications that some apparently idiomatic combinations do have **some** generality, even if not much. Give in, for example, has two meanings, corresponding to a transitive and an intransitive use, which are directly paralleled by the two readings of the verb surrender:

27. a. When he had run out of stones to throw he surrendered/gave in
    b. You must surrender your passport/give your passport in to the immigration office

The verb submit also has two similar uses. How much support of this nature do you need to stop being idiomatic?

EXERCISE 1

Go through the verbs in Table 6.1., testing them against the criteria elaborated here. Try to make precise any vagueness in the criteria which makes this difficult. How many verbs involve subregularities which I have not mentioned? How many verbs fit into the classes I have mentioned? Which phrasal verbs do you think are genuinely idiomatic?

Does this type of analysis work on other particles? Pairs such as in-out and on-off would be obvious ones to try.

6.4. PREDICTING PARTICLE POSITION

One of the defining characteristics of a phrasal verb is the separability of its two parts, especially noticeable when it is used transitively:

28. a. John ate up his dinner
    b. John ate his dinner up

Comparatively little attention, however, has been devoted to the question of the difference between these two forms. Yet on the whole languages tend not to contain multiple expressions of the same thing without utilising them to convey some distinction (although this distinction is not necessarily one which is purely semantic - i.e. which corresponds to different sets of truth conditions on sentences). It seems quite likely that, as this is a distinction of word order, a good candidate for determinant of the difference might be Functional Sentence Perspective (cf. section 3.3 for a discussion of this notion). In particular, we would expect to find intonational and contextual differences between sentences such as (28a) and those like (28b).

It is a commonplace observation in the literature that sentences which are ambiguous between phrasal verbs and prepositional verbs can often be distinguished in terms of their intonation, as prepositions are seldom stressed unless contrastive, while particles usually are stressed. This comes out most strongly, perhaps, in wh-questions where there can be no positional difference between the phrasal and prepositional verbs:

29. a. What did he look UP?
    b. What did he LOOK up?

The interpretation involved with dictionaries seems most natural with (29a), although it could clearly also be used contrastively ('no, I didn't say what did he look AT'). It would be extremely difficult to force (29b) even into a contrastive reading involving a phrasal verb. Note, incidentally, that this cannot be a case of emphasis being put on things which are less predictable than others. Though one can look things up and look things out, it is not possible to look things in, round, down, etc. So the particle up is not in fact in contrast with a great many other particles. But the preposition up is in contrast with down, round, at, into, from, etc. So this difference in stress placement appears to correlate fairly simply with an observation about the stressing of constituents: a stressed constituent is normally stressed on its last stressable word. If [look up] is a constituent (as it arguably is in phrasal verb combinations), stress will naturally fall on the particle; conversely, if look is stressed, a word which occurs after it is unlikely to be part of the same constituent, so following up must be a preposition.

This fact about particles, then, although fairly simply predictable, does not require functional sentence perspective as part of its explanation. But the predictability of particles does appear to have a role to play in their positioning as well. This emerges most clearly if we contrast a verb like do, which co-occurs with a large range of particles, with a verb like finish, which is not only fairly restricted in the range of particles which it accepts, but which also has such a clear meaning of resultativity that the particles which do occur with it do not add a great deal of meaning to the combination. We might therefore expect that <u>finish</u> would be happier with an unstressed particle than <u>do</u>, and that the unstressed particle would be unlikely to occur at the end of the sentence. The following sentences test this:

   30. a. He did UP his kitchen
       b. He did his kitchen UP
       c. ?He DID up his kitchen
       d. ??He DID his kitchen up
   31. a. ?He finished UP his dinner
       b. He finished his dinner UP
       c. He FINISHED up his dinner
       d. ?He FINISHED his dinner up

My intuitions are not crystal clear (are yours?), but on the whole the results appear to suggest that functional sentence perspective has some relevance. My reaction to (30c-d) is that either they appear to have a main verb missing (He DID do his kitchen up), or else <u>up</u> might be being used as a verb (He DID up his prices). In (31) it is the acceptability of (b) and the unacceptability of (d) which appear to require explanation. With (b) there seems to be stress on the fact that he did not just stop, leaving uneaten morsels on the plate, but actually left a clean plate; this is not naturally conveyed by (a) – perhaps because anyone who wished to lay emphasis on that aspect would naturally wish to put the crucially informative words in the position of highest prominence, the end of the sentence. The oddness of (d) is for the converse reason that it is perverse to place an unstressed and uninformative element in the position of greatest prominence. All of the examples that I have found in spontaneous speech with a clearly stressed particle have it final; but my sample can hardly be said to be representative.

    Another aspect of the prominence of particle-final position is the obligatory nature of this with all but the most contrastive pronouns:

   32. a. I did it up
       b. *I did up it

Another fact which may conceivably be related to this, although I can't quite see how, is that certain phrasal verbs with postposed particles sound much more polite than those with particles next to the verb:

   33. a. Take your coat off
       b. Take off your coat

Obviously tone of voice and other such factors are the crucial deciding factor in the 'friendliness' of a message, but (33a) is the sort of thing which you

might well say to a friend who has just come to
visit you, while (33b) has more the tone of the
mugger or immigration official.

There are other factors; certain specific
phrasal verb combinations separate quite reluctantly
(although not with pronouns):

34. a. They carried out the operation very
efficiently
    b. They carried it out very efficiently
    c. ??They carried the operation out very
efficiently

But it has to be said that a very substantial number
of cases where one or other variant appears in texts
could equally well have been formulated with the
other variant, at least as far as intuitions go.
This could be the sort of area where systematic
sociolinguistic or stylistic investigation could
repay effort (see chapter 10 for this type of
approach); but my own informal observations suggest
that a very substantial amount of speech would need
to be monitored before a sufficient quantity of
phrasal verbs could be accumulated to justify any
general quantitative conclusions. There is one
curious attempt in this vein; the Linguistic Atlas
of England has a table (Table S2) which plots over
the map of England responses to the question How
do you see in this room when it gets dark?. The conclusion is that 'The word order of We put the light
on is clearly dominant over most of the country
while We put on the light is confined to the South
West.' There seems to be a curious presupposition
here that speakers do not have both forms readily
available. The question of why one form might be
triggered rather than another is an interesting one,
but not likely to be revealed at all by a questionnaire such as this.

EXERCISE 2

Follow up this hypothesis on particle position with
a wider range of phrasal verbs to see whether it
makes sense. Intuitions may well be quite unreliable
here - if you can find examples in the speech you
hear around you, this could be quite useful.

READING - CHAPTER 6

Two major books worth reading on this
construction (apart from sections in the standard

grammars) are D. Bolinger <u>The Phrasal Verb</u>
(Harvard), and B. Fraser <u>The Verb-Particle</u>
<u>Combination in English</u> (Academic Press). Fraser's
book contains a list of such constructions, with
examples. More extensive, both in number of verbs
and in illustration, is D. Cowie & R. Mackin <u>The</u>
<u>Oxford Dictionary of English Idioms v.1. Phrasal and</u>
<u>Prepositional Verbs</u> (Oxford). The supposed dialect
division is claimed in H. Orton et al. <u>The</u>
<u>Linguistic Atlas of England</u>, London: Croom Helm,
1978.

Chapter Seven

NOMINALISATIONS

A simple sentence typically conveys - along with
other information - some sort of proposition; if
we wish to make that proposition into an argument of
a verb - i.e if we wish it to be embedded in
another sentence - there is a wide range of possibilities open to us, and these will be the subject
of the next four chapters. To take one of the most
hackneyed examples within recent discussion, the
proposition expressed in (1) can take the various
forms of (2) when it occurs as the subject of a
verb phrase like <u>should</u> <u>surprise</u> <u>you</u>, or the complement of some verbal element such as <u>think</u>, <u>dis-
approve</u> <u>of</u>, <u>prefer</u>, etc.:
  1. The enemy destroyed the city
  2. a. That the enemy destroyed the city
     b. For the enemy to destroy the city
     c. The enemy's destroying of the city
     d. The enemy's destroying the city
     e. The enemy destroying the city
     f. The enemy's destruction of the city
In subsequent chapters we shall be interested in
(a)-(e), which share the characteristic of being
(relatively) productive, in the sense that the possibility of their occurrence depends very little on
the specific verb which occurs in the embedded
proposition. Restrictions on the use of these forms
are more connected with their 'external' syntax -
the context in which they occur, the meaning they
are intended to convey, etc.
    In this chapter we shall be concerned with
cases such as (2f), which are not productive in the
same sense: it is an inherent property of <u>destroy</u>
that it is associated with the nominal form
<u>destruction</u>. Given a verb with phonological
similarities to <u>destroy</u>, it does not follow that it
will have a similar nominal form - cf. <u>enjoy</u>,

enjoyment, *enjuction. Conversely, given a nominal form similar to destruction, it does not follow that we will be able to reconstruct a verb on the same pattern as destroy - cf. construction, construct, *constroy. It does not even follow that a verb will have an associated nominal form of this type (cf. kill, have), or that a nominal form of this apparent type will correspond to an existing verb (cf. compunction, exposition). There are many aspects of the form of such nominals which are not susceptible to explanation at all; instead, many linguists have attempted to trace their history, involving borrowings from Latin, from Old French, etc. I have neither the erudition nor the inclination to do this; there are nonetheless some interesting general features to be drawn out of the data, and some implications for what relates to grammar and what to lexicon.

These forms have received a variety of names: I shall call them simply 'nominalisations', although 'derived nominal' is probably commoner. Strictly speaking, all of the forms in (2) are nominalisations, as they involve ways of giving nominal status to propositions. However, as we shall see, the other forms have names of their own, so I shall use 'nominalisation' just for type (f). I am not going to be concerned with means of nominalising adjectives (e.g. -ness, -ity), nor shall I consider those nominalising suffixes which cannot be used to derive abstract nouns of action or state - e.g. -er, which is fairly productively suffixed to verbs to indicate a person who does what the verb indicates. Just incidentally, however, it is worth noting that the usual 'counterexamples' to this productivity really are not; e.g. cooker is a thing which cooks, while cook is a person who cooks (for a living). However, in an appropriate context, cooker can also denote a person:

3. a. He is a proficient cooker of beans
   b. The cooker of books is always going to be found out

The basic nominalising devices that we shall be concerned with are: a whole family of suffixes having in common the ending -ion, the suffixes -ment, -al, -age, -ure, -ance (and its variants -ence, -ancy, -ency), and the null suffix - i.e. cases where the noun and verb are identical in form, sometimes differing in stress (e.g. torment), sometimes not (e.g. reply). These differ widely in productivity. However, they also differ in possible use in syntactic context, in meaning, etc. There are therefore three types of problem which we shall need to face in talking about nominalisations:

A. It is not altogether clear where we should draw the line in admitting that something is a nominalisation. In (2f), for instance, the nominalisation is surrounded by noun phrases, one corresponding to the subject of (1), and the other to its object. There are some nominal forms which do not allow the expression of NPs corresponding to the subject and object:

4. a. John hit Mary
   b. *John's hit of Mary

Do they then count as nominalisations?

B. There are semantic distinctions between nominalisations which have hardly been looked at in the literature on this subject. E.g. there is a distinction between those nominalisations which can refer to the result of the action of the corresponding verb (e.g. acquisition) and those which cannot (e.g. abdication). Nominalisations can sometimes be used to refer to the proposition as a fact, while at other times this is not possible. The whole area needs looking at.

C. It is clear that none of these forms is totally productive. However, this does not mean that there are no subregularities to be found. Once again, this is a field which is wide open to extensive investigation.

7.2. CRITERIA

There are several thousand word forms in an average English dictionary which are ambiguously verbal or nominal. Some of these we will recognise as verbs and their corresponding nominalisation (e.g. disregard, dislike), while with others we shall not for a moment accept such an analysis (e.g brick, hammer). In between these two extremes there will be a variety of words which behave like nominalisations in some ways, but not in others. Perhaps the primary criterion for status as a nominalisation is occurrence with two NPs representing subject and object (assuming that the verb is transitive):

5. a. John's disregard of everyone's advice was
         shocking
   b. *John's hammer of a nail in was impressive

Intuitively what seems to be going on here is that while disregard as a noun is derivative on its use as a verb, with hammer the reverse appears to be true - the noun is primary, and the verb acquires the meaning of the sort of things one does with a hammer. But there are nouns which seem intuitively to be derivative on verbs, but which do not occur in full nominalisations:

    6. a. *John's hit of his mother-in-law was vicious
      b. *His like of suet puddings is notorious

It is not just unsuffixed nominals which manifest such behaviour:

    7. a. *John's establishment of the truth shows his single-mindedness
      b. *Mary's astonishment of John amused us
      c. *John's information of the police did not go down well

It is clear that there can be no semantic restriction here, as replacement of this suffix with the more productive -ing renders the sentences of (7) acceptable.

There are other contexts in which nominalisations occur rather more freely. One such use is in 'verbo-nominal' constructions - combinations of a verb with an abstract noun which are generally equivalent in meaning to the verb from which the noun is derived. Give, take and have are the most frequent verbs in such constructions:

    8. a. John gave his mother-in-law a kick
      b. John's mother-in-law took a dislike to him
      c. John had an argument with his mother-in-law

Some of the abstract nouns which occur in this construction are remarkably limited in the range of contexts in which they occur. Think, for instance, occurs as a noun only in combinations such as:

    9. I'll have a think about it and tell you later

Other contexts of occurrence sound definitely odd:

    10. a. ?John's think did him a lot of good
      b. *You're depriving me of my daily think

The verbo-nominal construction can be seen as a 'lower bound' on nominalisation status, in the sense that nouns which do not occur in any other context may occur here, but also because there are many nominalisations capable of occurring with nominal 'subject' and 'object', but not in verbo-nominal constructions.

While both full nominalisations and verbo-nominal constructions have their own limits and constraints, their usefulness as criteria for nominalisation status is that they both cover much of the 'core' area of nominalisations, and neither of them allows words which are clearly not nominalisations. The shared 'core' can be seen from such

examples as:
11. a. Their approval of the plan was greeted
        with relief
    b. They gave their approval willingly
12. a. John's assertion of his rights surprised
        them
    b. He made an assertion which amazed
        everyone.
        It is not difficult to think of further crit-
eria which will distinguish deverbal nominalisations
from other nouns. E.g. just as verbs are modified by
adverbs of a variety of semantic classes, so nominalisations allow adjectives related to these various
types of adverbials - e.g. frequency or manner
adverbials:
13. a. They constantly destroy cities
    b. Their constant destruction of cities
14. a. He blatantly disregarded the rules
    b. His blatant disregard of the rules
15. *His frequent hammer
16. ??His cynical information
But while the detailed behaviour of adverbials is a
fascinating subject in its own right, the rough
outline sketched above is more or less what one
would expect given the distinction of 'real'
nominalisations from other nouns, and the major
concern of this section has been to distinguish such
nominalisations sufficiently for us to be able to
talk about them as a group. Furthermore, we would
inevitably be involved in complications relating to
the semantics of adverbials if we pursued this line;
for example, is the oddity of (15) and (16) merely a
semantic oddity? The behaviour of adverbials is
clearly significant in the syntax of nominalisations: but to bring it in as a criterion of nominalisation status would be to define the less obscure
in terms of the more obscure.

7.3. THE MEANINGS OF NOMINALISATIONS

Perhaps the most straightforward semantic distinction to make is between those nominalisations which
are capable of referring to entities of some sort
and those which are not. (Of course, given the
initial delimitation of section 7.2, all nominalisations that we are considering are usable in an
abstract sense as well.) Of those which can refer to
such entities there are two subclasses - those which
correlate roughly with the subject of the corresponding verb, and those which denote the result of the

action specified by the verb.

Those which correlate with the subject of the verb include such diverse words as the following:

administration, government, accommodation, adornment, advertisement, affliction, apparition, arrival, attendance, attraction.
-i.e. an administration adminstrates, an attraction attracts (people), and so on. There are, of course, additional semantic qualifications to be made about many of these words. <u>Administrations</u> and <u>governments</u> are bodies of people whose official function is to administer/govern. An <u>advertisement</u> is a piece of paper, a jingle, a form of words, but very seldom a person, although cf.

17. He's the best advertisement this place has got

It is never the same as an <u>advertiser</u>, however. <u>Arrival</u> is not entirely restricted to babies (as in (18)), but it is only very restrictedly used in other contexts:

18. Their latest arrival weighs nine pounds

All of these words have restrictions of various sorts imposed on them: there are certain possible regularities among them, but the overall impression is of rather little regularity.

Nominalisations which denote the result of an action include:

abbreviation, abstraction, accomplishment, accumulation, achievement, acquisition, adaptation, addition, affirmation, allocation, appointment, etc.

On the whole there is a good correlation between these and the object of the corresponding verb, but this is not perfect, and the term 'result' seems more appropriate. E.g. <u>abbreviation</u> denotes not what is abbreviated, but what it is abbreviated to. Similarly with <u>adaptation</u>; or <u>condensation</u>. These forms seem much less idiosyncratic than the corresponding subject forms. Whenever there is a resultative verb, from which some concrete result emerges, then it seems that the nominalisation is capable of expressing that result.

Among nominalisations expressing abstract notions, there are some further distinctions of meaning which are fairly subtle, but which are quite important (and will be seen to be of further importance in later chapters). Take a sentence such as (19):

19. The abolition of the House of Lords will take a little time

Clearly what will take time here is the **action**, or

process, of abolition. Contrast this with (20):

20. The abolition of the House of Lords cheered the Labour Party immensely

Here it is less clear what is at issue: however it seems that it is the **fact** of abolition, or the **manner** of abolition which is cheering. Not all nominalisations as we define them here have all of these interpretations:

21. His work on that problem earned him a lot of respect

There is no interpretation of (21) as 'the fact that he worked on that problem ...', even though this is an intelligible thing to say. A manner or result interpretation seems more plausible, i.e. it can be interpreted in either of the following ways:

21'. a. The way he worked on that problem earned him a lot of respect

b. The published results of his work on that problem earned him a lot of respect

I would not wish to claim specifically either that these two interpretations exhaust the possibilities, or that this is a genuine ambiguity (as opposed to a sentence which is vague between different interpretations). However, these two possibilities seem particularly salient.

So in relation to abstract nominalisations we can distinguish action (19), fact (20) and manner (20, 21) interpretations ((21'b) is not an abstract interpretation, of course). Two types of factor influence possible interpretations – the inherent nature of the nominalisation and the external syntactic or semantic context in which it occurs. Some of the relationships between nominalising suffixes and the inherent properties of the nominalisations will be examined in the next section. There are also, of course, purely semantic factors to be taken into consideration; e.g. <u>dislike</u>, <u>abhorrence</u>, <u>amazement</u>, etc. are incompatible with both action and manner interpretations by virtue of denoting attitudes. In terms of the tripartite distinction mentioned here, the sentences of (22) are unambiguous:

22. a. His dislike of whisky is well known

b. His amazement was quite evident

The external factors constraining interpretation can be seen quite clearly in (19) – the predicate <u>will take a little time</u> requires that the subject be something capable of temporal extension, which excludes manners and facts. In (21), by contrast, it is the nature of <u>work</u> which excludes the fact interpretation – many unsuffixed nominalisations do not have such an interpretation.

EXERCISE 1

I have relied on a distinction of 'abstract' NPs and NPs denoting 'entities of some sort'. Can this distinction be made more precise and still work?

EXERCISE 2

Examine this semantic typology of nominalisations, and try to extend it, or make it more precise, by considering a variety of other contexts in which nominalisations can occur (such as those below), and a variety of nominalisations in each context;

    ____ was a welcome step
    the prospect of ____ is intriguing
    the result of ____ was ...
    etc.

Table 7.1 is a reference list of suffixal nominalisations culled from a single letter of the alphabet in a small dictionary; you may find this of use in examining the occurrence and intepretation of nominalisations, although it may also be useful to go outside this list.

7.4. SOME POSSIBLE REGULARITIES

Attempts have occasionally been made to find a purely formal basis on which to differentiate the different suffixes used for nominalisations, but these attempts have been almost uniformly unsuccessful. Even fairly well-founded suggestions tend to show some exceptions: e.g. the prefixes <u>en</u>- and <u>be</u>- clearly favour the use of the suffix -<u>ment</u> in nominalisations (cf. <u>enjoyment</u>, <u>enforcement</u>, <u>bereavement</u>, <u>bedevilment</u>, etc.), but it is certainly not true that the mere existence of one of these prefixes guarantees the possibility of a nominalisation in -<u>ment</u> (cf. <u>encode</u>, <u>encounter</u>, <u>engrave</u>, <u>enumerate</u>, <u>betroth</u>, <u>betray</u>, <u>belong</u>, <u>beatify</u>, etc.) Verbs which end in a suffix -<u>ate</u> have corresponding nominalisations in -<u>ation</u>, but of course there are verbs which end in -<u>ate</u> which do not so nominalise (e.g. <u>restate</u>, <u>berate</u>), the reason being that the -<u>ate</u> here is not a suffix but part of the root. There seems also to be an extremely good correlation between verbs which end in -<u>ify</u> and nominalisations which end in -<u>ification</u>, and verbs which end in -<u>ise</u> and nominalisations in -<u>isation</u>. Aronoff has claimed

Table 7.1.   Some nominalisations

---

abbreviation	amalgamation	abandonment
abdication	ambition	abasement
abduction	amplification	abashment
aberration	amputation	abatement
abjuration	animadversion	abetment
abnegation	annexation	accompaniment
abolition	anticipation	accomplishment
abomination	apparition	achievement
abortion	application	acknowledgement
abrasion	appreciation	adjournment
abrogation	apprehension	adjudgement
absolution	appropriation	adjustment
absorption	approximation	admonishment
abstention	arbitration	adornment
abstraction	ascription	advancement
acceleration	assertion	advertisement
accentuation	assignation	agreement
accommodation	assimilation	alignment
accumulation	association	allurement
accusation	assumption	amazement
acetification	attention	amendment
acquisition	attestation	amusement
action	attraction	announcement
adaptation	attribution	appeasement
addiction	augmentation	appointment
addition		apportionment
adduction		argument
adhesion		armament
adjudication		arraignment
adjuration		arrangement
administration		ascertainment
admiration		assessment
admonition		assignment
adoption		assortment
adoration		assuagement
adulation	abhorrence	astonishment
aeration	abstinence	atonement
affiliation	acceptance	attachment
affirmation	acquiescence	attainment
affliction	admittance	
agglomeration	allowance	
agglutination	annoyance	
aggression	appearance	acquittal
alienation		approval
allegation		arrival
alleviation		
allocation	alteration	
allusion	alternation	assemblage

that -ation is, exceptionally, excluded when a root
ends in a 'palatal strident' ([ʃ], [tʃ] or [dʒ])
because of a general phonotactic principle of English that two coronal stridents do not come in a
row. With words of this sort, -ment is fairly productive, he claims (cf. judgement, attachment, establishment, etc.). This is largely true; but we cannot
conclude from this that any verb ending in one of
these segments will have a nominalisation in -ment
- cf. *changement, *watchment, *crashment, etc.
(Nor, incidentally, is the 'phonotactic principle'
without exceptions - cf. magician, Cheshire, etc.)
What we have here are **partial** regularities.

There is also a largish number of cases where
either two different nominalisations are formed from
the same verb (as in the list (23)), or else verbs
with very similar endings form different types of
nominalisation (as in (24)):

23. admonition - admonishment
    referral - reference
    assignment - assignation
    abstinence - abstention
    proposal - proposition
24. establishment - abolition - diminution
    involvement - evolution
    achievement - reception
    information - adornment

There are also cases of semantic irregularity; one
meaning of contain, for instance, correlates semantically with containment and not at all with content-
ion (which relates to contend), while detain and
detention are obviously semantically related. In the
face of such diversity it seems perverse to say that
there is any completely regular formal relation to
be established between verbs and their nominalisations in English. This is further reinforced by the
fact that many of the same relationships hold in
French and/or Latin, and such regularities as there
are in the English data appear to be entirely derivative from regularities which hold in these languages.

However it is possible to establish tendencies
in the syntactic and semantic behaviour of nominalisations of different types. In particular it
appears that the three majority types form a hier-
archy which covers both the semantic factor of having a 'fact'-interpretation, and the syntactic
factor of being capable of occurring as full nominalisations. Those nominalisations which end in -ion
are most natural in both of these uses, -ment is
rather less natural, while the suffixless nominalis-

ations are the least capable of such use. This is not to say that all -ion forms are identical in behaviour, different in some consistent way from all -ment forms. What is meant, rather, is that the number of regularly derived forms in -ion which do not occur as full nominalisations, or with a possible fact interpretation, is rather small, while the number of -ment forms which do not occur in these same uses is rather larger. There is a further difference which emphasises the more purely formal nature of the relationship between -ion nominalisations and their verbs: this is that -ion nominalisations more frequently cover the full range of uses of their verb than do -ment forms. E.g. corresponding to the sentences in (25), we find the nominalisations of (26), but only (27a) has a corresponding nominalisation:

25. a. John applied for a job
    b. John applied his learning very successfully
    c. John applied glue to the surface
26. a. John's application for a job
    b. John's very successful application of his learning
    c. John's application of glue to the surface
27. a. John accompanied Mary on the piano
    b. John accompanied Mary to the cinema
28. a. John's accompaniment of Mary on the piano
    b. *John's accompaniment of Mary to the cinema

This is not to say that -ion forms cannot be semantically idiosyncratic as well: application, in the sense of 'hard work' is an example of that. And of course many of the forms which can be found in Table 7.1 or any other relatively indiscriminate compilation of such forms, are arbitrary to some degree either formally, semantically, or both.

It is not at all clear how regular or irregular the minor patterns of nominalisation are. If you look in a reverse dictionary (one organised in alphabetical order starting with the last letter of each word), it usually becomes fairly obvious that there is a pattern of some sort, the only problem being to decide how significant the pattern is. E.g. looking at the suffix -al shows that it is only preceded by the letters r, s (phonologically representing both /s/ and /z/), t, u, v, w and y. (How very odd that such an almost neat chunk of the alphabet should be chosen!) Many of these words are not common (requital, suppressal, discontinual, indrawal, receival, demurral, etc.), although some are perfectly common (e.g. <u>disposal</u>, <u>retrieval</u>, <u>acquittal</u>, <u>betrayal</u>). It is clear that the suffix -<u>al</u> is not productive in the sense that new words can be freely coined with it (as, for example, the formation of nouns in -<u>ness</u> from adjectives is productive). Yet it is surely a fact about English that the suffix is limited in particular ways; many dictionaries do not contain the word <u>referral</u>; it is only in the Supplement to the OED, with 1934 given as its first use. I found this surprising, but could hardly have been surprised at the absence of forms which do not fit in the normal environment for this suffix - e.g. *<u>decidal</u>, *<u>rebuffal</u>, *<u>designal</u>.

There is currently some disagreement among linguists concerned with word formation as to what their proper subject of study is. One view is that **existing** words - usually taken to be those occurring in dictionaries, although this is by no means necessary - are the only legitimate interest of the derivational morphologist. There is very clear evidence, however (mainly from languages with a richer morphological system than English) that speakers use word formation rules productively and unpredictably. Dictionaries **codify** usage, largely ignoring the spontaneous creations of informal speech. It is quite likely that speakers using relatively formal style do not make the same use of such devices. Furthermore, the development of a language such as English in its codified form is constrained by its international status, by the wide variety of dialects within it, by formal schooling, etc. But there is no reason why linguists should not look at productive use of derivational morphology, or at speakers' intuitions as to what is an acceptable use of word formation devices. From that point of view, word formation is concerned with all **possible** words. For a morphological device to be unproductive, it is not sufficient that the OED not list any new formations of that type since 1543; speakers must refuse to countenance any new formations. Productivity, like most other notions in linguistics, can be seen as a continuum, with -<u>al</u> certainly in the lower half, but by no means at the extreme of unproductivity.

EXERCISE 3

Look at one or more of the 'minor' nominalising suffixes listed in section 1.
- Are there general phonological, semantic or

syntactic constraints on this suffix?
- If so, test for these in the following way:
take a small list (e.g. 20) of forms divided into
four subclasses:
    - attested in dictionaries and familiar to you
    - attested in dictionaries but unfamiliar to
you
    - not attested, but conforming to the con-
straints you have found
    - not attested, and not conforming to the
constraints you have found
Try any of the following ways of questioning
native speakers:
    - directly; "Is suppressal a word of English?"
    - indirectly; "Is the following a normal English
sentence: The suppressal of the riots is still continuing?"
    - "What is the nominal form of suppress?"
    - "If suppression wasn't the nominal form of
suppress, what else could be?"
(Clearly in these latter cases you would need to
ensure that people knew what a 'nominal form' was.)
[Alternatively ask any type of question which
seems feasible to you.]

READING - CHAPTER 7

There's not a lot of work done on this, even though
nominalisations have been a big theoretical issue in
the past. The 'standard' work on English word
formation is H. Marchand Categories and Types of
English Word Formation (Heidelberg). Reverse
dictionaries (alphabetised from the end of a word
rather than the beginning) are most useful tools in
morphological research; the one used here is J. L.
Dolby & H. L. Resnikoff The English Word Speculum
Mouton 5 vols (vols 3,4 and 5 all have reverse word
lists, all organised in different ways, but usable.)
A recent textbook with much relevant information
both on word formation in general and nominal
derivatives of verbs in particular is L. Bauer Word
Formation, Cambridge, 1983. The most important work
on morphology specifically in current generative
grammar is M. Aronoff Word Formation in Generative
Grammar, Cambridge, Mass: MIT Press, 1976.

Chapter Eight

ING

There are at least three distinct forms in English
which involve adding the suffix -ing to a verb stem
- the participle, the gerund and the action nominal.
Participles (which we shall not be further concerned
with except insofar as they may be confused with
gerunds) are adjectival forms of the verb, and, like
adjectives, they occur after the verb be (the progressive aspect) and before and after nouns (exhibit-
ing some of the same variation as shown by passive
participles in this respect - cf. chapter 5.):
    1. a. John is mending his bicycle
       b. The crying baby had fallen down
       c. The baby crying had fallen down
The gerund and the action nominal are both ways of
nominalising sentences (using the term 'nominalise'
in its broad - and not necessarily transformational
- sense). However, gerundive constructions have many
more of the properties of sentences than action
nominals, and many fewer of the properties of nouns.
The 'subject' of an action nominal, for instance, is
always possessive, while the subject of a gerund may
or may not be (and if it is not, it occurs in the
'oblique' case if it is a pronoun):
    2. a. John's mending of the bicycle was inept
       b. *John mending of the bicycle was inept
    3. a. John's mending the bicycle is odd
       b. John mending the bicyle is odd
       c. Him mending the bicycle is odd
As can be seen from (2), the 'object' of the action
nominal always occurs with the preposition of, while
the 'object' of the gerund occurs in the same form
as it would in the corresponding sentence. Like
nouns, action nominals are modified by adjectives,
while gerunds are modified by adverbs:
    4. a. John's inept mending of the bicycle
       b. *John's ineptly mending of the bicycle

     5. a. John's ineptly mending the bicycle
       b. *John's inept mending the bicycle
The situation is complicated slightly by the fact that adverbs are better than expected with action nominals when they occur at the end of the construction, and especially when they are prepositional phrases:
     6. a. ?John's mending of the bicycle ineptly
       b. John's mending of the bicycle on Saturday
However, this can also be related to the fact that adverbials as in (6b) occur also with other nominals:
     7. a. John's death on Saturday was a great blow
       b. The prize on Saturday is a trip to
           Blackpool
       c. The newspaper on Monday had an interesting
           article in it
Action nominals, but not gerunds, occur with articles:
     8. a. The mending of the bicycle by John
       b. *The mending the bicycle (by John)
As a final difference, note that gerunds may occur with a variety of auxiliaries to indicate aspect and/or tense, while action nominals do not occur in such contexts:
     9. a. John's having mended the bicycle amazed us
       b. John's being given a book amazed us
    10. a. *John's having mended of the bicycle
         amazed us
       b. *John's being given of a book amazed us
There are therefore numerous differences between gerunds and action nominals. Note, however, that when used intransitively and without adverbial or adjectival modification or an article, there is regular ambiguity between the two forms:
    11. a. John's running impressed everyone
       b. John's looking at dirty films was
         disapproved of
These forms are genuinely ambivalent: we can talk of 'John's careful running' or of 'John's carefully running'. I shall argue later that they are also genuinely ambiguous. But it is as well to be aware of the fact that this unelaborated intransitive use conflates two forms, and is therefore not of much assistance in any attempt to distinguish between them.

    It is worth pointing out here that, both in form and in function, action nominals are very close to derived nominals (i.e. those considered in chapter 7). Thus, all of the nominal features of action nominals are also characteristic of derived

nominals, and none of the verbal ones are:
12. a. his abrupt removal
    b. *his abruptly removal
13. The removal of the furniture
It might be expected that coordination possibilities would throw some light on this. Of course it would not be surprising to find gerundive constructions, action nominals and derived nominals conjoined as wholes, given that they are all NPs: such things do indeed occur in texts:
14. There is a lapse of almost exactly a year between Mary's leaving him and the publication of this book
What should be impossible is the sharing of 'subject' or 'object' NPs in coordination between gerund and action nominals, while between action nominal and derived nominal it might be expected to be acceptable:
15. a. his publication of one book and writing of another
    b. *?his publication of one book and writing another
    c. *his publishing one book and writing of another
Insofar as my judgements are clear, they seem to confirm these expectations. What **is** certain is that the types of constructions which would give evidence one way or the other are quite infrequent in texts - i.e. normal use of language. Gerunds and action nominals alike are very rare in spoken English (except for the adverbial use of gerunds), and such constructions with coordinated parts are rare any-where.

EXERCISE 1

Look at a variety of possible coordinations of gerundive constructions, action nominals and derived nominals. Are there any regularities which you can discern among these compatibilities and incompat-ibilities?

8.2. THE RANGE OF GERUNDS AND ACTION NOMINALS

The gerund is the most productive of the various forms for deriving nominal elements from verbs. Only the modal verbs (<u>may</u>, <u>can</u>, <u>must</u>, etc.) among English verbs do not form a gerund, and that is simply because they do not form any non-finite form of the verb. Indeed, it has been suggested that they are simply morphologically defective just as, for instance, some Latin verbs have incomplete paradigms. The action nominal is also productive in English, but its productivity is confined within narrower bounds. It is called 'action nominal' because it is unhappy with verbs which do not denote an action:

16. a. ?John's liking of Mary is strange
    b. ??John's appreciating of the concert knew no bounds
    c. *John's weighing of twenty stone disgusted her

It can reasonably be argued that this semantic selectivity of the action nominal also accounts for the fact that it does not occur with auxiliary verbs, as auxiliary verbs do not denote actions. Other than this restriction, action nominals can be formed from any verb.

There is one restriction on the occurrence of the gerund which appears to depend on factors other than the inherent nature of the connection between gerund and verb. You may have noted that I did not illustrate the use of the gerund with the progressive auxiliary; if I had done, the result would have sounded odd:

17. *John's being mending the bicycle is odd

However, it is not merely progressives that sound odd: many combinations of two words ending in -ing sound odd:

18. a. *John's liking eating chips is typical of him
    b. *I was surprised at John's coming dancing

The precise nature of the constraint here has been the subject of much debate; some such combinations sound better than they 'ought to':

19. John's suggesting eating chips was welcomed

But whatever the formulation required, it would appear that no specific restriction on the gerund is required.

There is some debate in the theoretical literature as to how the gerund and the action nominal relate to the distinction between active and passive sentences. For our purposes, it is sufficient to note that the gerund is equipped with the same formal distinctions as a verb:

20. a. John's being hit by Mary (shocked us)
    b. Mary's hitting John (shocked us)

The action nominal is rather more of a problem. The following variations are found:

21. a. John's killing of the duck

b. The killing of the duck by John

c. ?The duck's killing by John

The action nominal of (21a) fits the active sentence in a rather natural way. (21c) would be just like the passive sentence, but it is not altogether natural as a structure at all. Note that this constitutes a difference between the action nominal and the derived nominal, as the following data shows:

22. a. the destruction/destroying of the town

b. the town's destruction

c. *the town's destroying

In contrast to the other two, (21b) is not altogether like either the active or the passive. It may be that the suggestion which has often been made in recent literature that the syntax of the nominal is quite separate from the syntax of the sentence is applicable in this case also. Given such an approach, one would clearly try to relate the syntax of nominals such as (21) to the syntax of simple nouns with possessive modifiers. However, I shall leave further consideration of this approach to the final section of this chapter.

Note that possible confusions of the gerund and the participle exist and need to be borne in mind. E.g. a sentence like (23) is ambiguous between participial and gerundive interpretation:

23. I was surprised at the man eating candy floss

What one is surprised at is either the man or the situation. Particular syntactic contexts favour either one or the other interpretation, eg:

24.a. The man eating candy floss was rather peculiar

b. I went away without the man being notified

(24a) suggests very strongly that it was the man, rather than the situation of his eating candy floss, that was peculiar; (24b), on the other hand, suggests that it was the situation of the man not being notified which held when I went away, rather than that I went away without a particular man. It is possible to conceive of situations where the rejected interpretation is required, but such situations do not immediately spring to mind on hearing (24), and the normal interpretations are so strongly preferred as to make these sentences unambiguous, for all practical purposes. The point to note is that the preferred interpretation depends less upon the internal syntax of the gerund/participial phrase than on the context in which they are embedded and on the likelihood of particular situations. This should make us rather cautious about coming to general conclusions about the contexts in which the gerund occurs.

One of the major problems with action nominals, as with nominalisations, is knowing where to draw the line in establishing them as a coherent class of elements. This can be illustrated with examples such as the following:

25. a. John's feeling of insecurity is becoming a serious problem
    b. ??John feels insecurity
    c. John feels a certain insecurity
    d. ??John's feeling of a certain insecurity

(25a) has all the appearances of being a straight-forward action nominal. The problem is that the corresponding sentence is highly dubious in accept-ability; if the sentence is manipulated to make it more acceptable, the nominal becomes correspondingly less acceptable. The problem is compounded by the fact that feeling does a few things which are quite untypical of action nominals: it occurs with an indefinite article (a feeling of insecurity) and in the plural (feelings of insecurity). There is also the semantic point that insecurity is the feeling, quite unlike the 'normal' object of action nominals. In this respect feeling is more like state (John's state of insecurity). (25a) is also untypical of action nominals in that there is no corresponding structure with postposed 'agent':

26. *The feeling of insecurity by John

There is also the small point that feel (in this sense, as opposed to the active tactile sense) is not an action. All things considered it would appear to be better to analyse feeling as a simple noun, rather than as an action nominal.

A number of other -ing forms also behave in somewhat deviant ways. Feeling is not alone in hav-ing indefinite and plural forms; a relatively sem-antically coherent group of elements denoting violent physical assault can also have these forms - e.g. beatings, floggings, muggings, shootings, kill-ings, etc. However, with these nouns there are all the normal features of action nominals as well as these relatively deviant features. This is not surprising if we assume that these are separate lexical items which just happen to have the form of action nominals. As the formation of action nominals is productive, we would expect that the idiosyn-cratic lexical nouns in -ing would be paralleled by action nominals formed productively from verbs, and this is indeed what we find. We would also expect that not all semantically similar elements would show this idiosyncratic use, and this expectation is also fulfilled; e.g. although <u>murdering</u> can be used as an action nominal, it does not occur in plural or indefinite form, the simple noun <u>murder</u> being used instead. Similarly <u>backing</u> can appear as a regular action nominal or idiosyncratically; in the first case it is likely to be replaceable by a near-synonym action nominal, while in its idiosyncratic use it cannot:

27. a. Their backing of the plan was vital to its success
    b. The manager asked for their backing
    c. Their supporting of the plan was vital to its success
    d. *The manager asked for their supporting
    e. The manager asked for their support

In all of these cases, therefore, we find that the regular action nominal is usually interchangeable with another action nominal, while the homophonous nouns in -<u>ing</u> which are used in a rather deviant way may be interchangeable only with simple nouns. There is nothing to be surprised at here. Some forms in -<u>ing</u> are now independent lexical items, with semantic specifications quite independent of any verb. At the same time, given the productivity (within limits) of the action nominal, the same form may occur as an action nominal with a meaning totally derivative of that of the verb it is based on. So we have a simple case of homonymy which, although historically going back to a single form, cannot be revealingly analysed in this way synchronically. Other idiosyncratic -<u>ing</u>s include <u>beginning(s)</u>, <u>liking</u>, etc. and there is further evidence of semantic subgroupings – e.g. pejorative words for speech (<u>ramblings</u>, <u>vapourisings</u>, <u>rabbitings-on</u>) or words for accumulated money (<u>takings</u>, <u>savings</u>, <u>earnings</u>).

8.3. THE MEANING OF GERUNDS AND ACTION NOMINALS

There is an ambiguity which is commonly noted in sentences such as (28):

28. I was surprised at his driving

The ambiguity is between an interpretation as in (29a) and one as in (29b):

29. a. I was surprised at the fact that he was driving
    b. I was surprised at the way he was driving

A continuation such as 'given that he had a broken

leg' on (28) is naturally compatible with the reading of (29a), while a continuation such as 'when I
went to London with him' more or less forces (29b).
It is to be noted that (28) is one of those sentences which are ambivalent between a gerundive and
an action nominal interpretation, as pointed out
above. It would therefore seem natural to hypothesise that the two different readings of (28) should
correlate with the two different constructions which
it exemplifies. This turns out to be the case. (30a)
is only interpretable as (29a) (mutatis mutandis),
and (30b) as (29b); (30c) is also interpretable as
(29a):

    30. a. I was surprised at his driving the car
        b. I was surprised at his driving of the car
        c. I was surprised at him driving the car

It would therefore appear that (30a), and other
gerunds, can only be interpreted as referring to
facts (in the semantic typology outlined in the last
chapter), while action nominals such as (30b) typically refer to the manner in which an action is
carried out. It would be amazing if things were that
simple, but this distinction is a useful one as a
frame of reference. Note incidentally that this
distinction would be sufficient to explain the
restriction of action nominals to actions: only
actions naturally occur with manner adverbs, for
instance, so it is natural to assume that a form
which refers to the manner in which something is
done has to refer to an action rather than, e.g., a
state.

    One can use syntactic frames, just as in
section 7.3, to test the semantic distinctiveness of
the two forms. E.g. the predicate '___ was a dreadful sight' could hardly be used appropriately of a
fact; neither could '___ was rather prolonged'.
Facts are not the sorts of things which are visible,
nor do they have temporal extension. A manner interpretation is virtually forced by a predicate such as
'___ was totally botched'. It is difficult to force
a fact interpretation with a particular syntactic
context, but clearly a verb such as shock is capable
of having facts as subject, though also acts and
manners. My intuitions give the following pattern:

    31. a. ??His driving the car was a dreadful
            sight
        b. His driving of the car was a dreadful
            sight
    32. a. *His driving the car was rather prolonged
        b. ?His driving of the car was rather
            prolonged

33. a. *His driving the car was totally botched
    b. His driving of the car was totally botched
34. a. His driving the car shocked us
    b. His driving of the car shocked us

When we introduce into the comparison the gerund without a possessive marker on the subject NP, the results are not identical to the judgements obtained from possessive gerunds. In particular, (35) seems perfectly acceptable, in contrast to (31a) - cf. section 8.4 for more discussion:

35. Him driving the car was a dreadful sight

Further differences are found with subjectless gerunds. One of the initial points of difference between subjectless gerunds and subjectless action nominals is that the former are normally 'controlled' - i.e. the subject must be interpreted as identical to some (overt or understood) NP in the main clause, while with action nominals this is not necessarily the case:

36. a. The emperor enjoyed torturing prisoners
    b. The emperor enjoyed the torturing of prisoners

(36a) must be understood as saying that the emperor took part in the torturing himself, while (36b) is quite consistent with the emperor merely being an appreciative observer of other people torturing prisoners (although it could also be interpreted in the same way as (36a) is). The notion of 'control' mentioned here differs in certain respects from that used elsewhere. In particular, what I am referring to is the **semantic** property that the subject of the gerund must be understood as identical to a specific participant (usually the experiencer) of the main clause state of affairs. E.g. in sentences such as:

37. a. Shooting foxes is fun
    b. Shooting foxes is forbidden

the subject of <u>shooting</u> must be interpreted as identical to the experiencer of the fun or the person to whom the forbidding is addressed. With the action nominal, this interpretation is possible as well, and may turn out to be the only possible interpretation by virtue of the situation described, but there is no **linguistic** reason why identity of this sort should hold, and therefore, if there is an alternative possible interpretation, the action nominal will allow this.

38. a. The shooting of foxes is fun
    b. The shooting of foxes is forbidden

In (a), the fun described may be fun for the observer, while in (b), it is necessarily the case that the forbidding is being addressed to the person (capable of) doing the shooting, rather than, say, an observer. But this has nothing to do with linguistic properties of these sentences: the notion of forbidding requires that there be an action that someone is forbidden to do, and hence any phrase describing an action which occurs in this slot will be interpreted as such. However, there are certain cases where the subjectless gerund appears to occur with no controller - cf. the following newspaper examples:

39. a. To be sure, combatting inflation is a necessary task

    b. The economy is not a cake which governments can cut at will, and one effect of curtailing growth was to reduce the use of capacity to about 89 per cent

The fact remains that the vast majority of uses of the subjectless gerund involve necessary coreference with some NP. The subjectless gerund can sometimes occur in contexts where no other form of the gerund is allowed:

40. a. Eating crisps is forbidden in church

    b. The eating of crisps is forbidden in church

    c. The eating of crisps by children is forbidden in church

    d. *Children's eating crisps is forbidden in church

    e. *Children eating crisps is forbidden in church

(Note that here it is necessary to assume that forbid has an 'understood' indirect object which controls the subject position of the subjectless gerund in (40a).) This is also true of the common adverbial use of gerunds:

41. a. They got in by forcing the lock

    b. *They got in by a policeman('s) forcing the lock

EXERCISE 2

Subjectless gerunds and action nominals often occur as complements of verbs (as in (36a&b) above). In some cases you will find that one or the other of these constructions is unacceptable as complement of a verb, while in other cases you will find that they differ in interpretation. Try them as complements of a variety of verbs (or verb + preposition), and try to determine which factors affect their acceptability and interpretation. (You might start with verbs such as <u>like</u>, <u>start</u>, <u>watch</u>, <u>participate</u> <u>in</u>, <u>object</u> <u>to</u>, etc.)

8.4. POSSESSIVE AND NON-POSSESSIVE

Another general problem which arises, and which I have already mentioned, is the difference between the gerund with the possessive marker on its subject and the same form without. It would appear that the non-possessive version has a wider semantic potentiality, and therefore occurs in constructions where the possessive variant does not occur. In certain cases the possessive variant expresses a meaning that the non-possessive cannot express - that the speaker is referring to the action specified in the gerundive construction **as a fact** (this is usually termed 'factive' meaning). There are, however, cases where the avoidance of ambiguity (with the participial construction) may be seen as leading to a strong preference for the possessive variant:

    42. a. The man eating chips disgusted the old lady

        b. The man's eating chips disgusted the old lady

(42a) is perfectly acceptable, but I would interpret it most naturally as a participial construction - i.e. the phrase <u>eating chips</u> is inserted so that the hearer can identify which man is at issue, and it is the man, rather than the fact that he is eating chips, which the old lady finds disgusting.

    Think of the nature of the possessive construction in general in English. We are concerned in particular with three possible variants:

    43. a. John's friend

        b. a friend of John

        c. a friend of John's

(Of course there is also the possibility <u>one of John's friends</u>, but we can ignore that at the moment.) The various factors that we have looked at in chapter 3 in relation to the passive seem to be relevant to at least some degree in the possessive as well. (Note, incidentally, that there is now considerable consensus that these factors determine basic aspects of sentence structure in a wide variety of languages.)

    A. Animates (especially humans) favour <u>'s</u>, while inanimates (especially abstracts) favour <u>of</u>:

    44. a. John's pen

        b. *the pen of John

        c. *punishment's purpose

          d. the purpose of punishment
    B. Longer NPs favour of:
    45. a. ??the man standing over there's brother
        b. the brother of the man standing over
           there
        c. *the brother of John
One contributing point here is that postnominal
modifiers often fit uneasily with the 's genitive,
which is at its most acceptable when immediately
following a head noun - cf. the following examples
from Schachter where even the possible form of the
possessive is unclear:
    46. a. Both of them being stolen was a shock
        b. *Both of them's being stolen was a shock
        c. *Both of their being stolen was a shock
This does not merely relate to -ing forms:
    47. a. the life of every one of us is at stake
        b. *every one of our life is at stake
        c. every one of our lives is at stake
           (different meaning)
    C. Less clearly, indefinites seem to favour of:
    48. a. I saw something that looked like the
           book's cover
        b. I saw something that looked like the
           cover of the book
        c. ??I saw something that looked like a
           book's cover
        d. I saw something that looked like the
           cover of a book
    D. Emphasis (and so presumably Functional sent-
ence perspective) appears to be relevant to this
distinction also. Short and highly unemphatic noun
phrases (e.g. personal pronouns) do not occur in the
postposed non-possessive form:
    49. a. a friend of mine
        b. *a friend of me
Emphatic noun phrases (e.g. wh-phrases in echo questions), by contrast, do not occur in the postposed
possessive form:
    50. a. He's a friend of WHO?
        b. *He's a friend of WHOSE?
As we have seen in the discussion in chapter 3, this
factor also relates to length, and to definiteness.
    Where both of and 's occur (as in (43c) above),
animacy and definiteness appear to be favouring
factors, but long NPs appear to avoid this construction:
    51. a. a friend of John's
        b. a friend of the man's
        c. ??a friend of a man's
        d. ??a friend of the man you saw's

e. ??a wheel of the car's
f. *a wheel of a car's
g. a friend of his
h. *a wheel of its

The question that then arises, given that we accept for the moment that factors of this sort are relevant to a determination of the possessive in general, is how this carries over to the gerundive construction which has the option of possessive noun phrase or not.

Note first of all that the paradigms we are talking about are really quite different from those of the simple possessive noun phrase: compare (43), above with the following:

52. a. John's driving
    b. the driving of John
    c. *the driving of John's
    d. John driving

The simple possessive noun phrase does not have anything corresponding to (d), at least in any direct way; note, however, that constructions such as <u>table top</u> or <u>boot lace</u> are rather similar to possessive constructions, and the 'possessor' is invariably indefinite, non-specific, inanimate, short, etc. The ungrammaticality of (52c) shows that there is no direct correspondence in that form either. What we **do** find in common is two general features - the preposed or postposed genitive construction, which occurs in both ordinary NPs and action nominals, and the 's-marked/unmarked distinction, which we find in both postposed genitive constructions with ordinary NPs, and with gerundive constructions (preposed). The question is: are there any general properties of these two oppositions which unite these different constructions in which they are relevant? Taking animacy first, this is clearly relevant in the choice of 's form, although not nearly so rigidly as is the case with ordinary NPs. Inanimate NPs frequently seem rather forced when they are marked with 's, and there are a few which are quite impossible with 's:

53. We went outside because of the room(?'s) being bugged
54. I was amazed at it(??s) being so well attended
55. There was no sign of there(*'s) having been a struggle

(This last example is Schachter's.) Animate nouns simply tend to seem a little more colloquial without any ending:

56. John coming is a good idea

Note in this connection that gerunds and action nominals are extraordinarily rare in normal spontaneous conversation, although much more frequent in journalese and more formal styles. There is also a certain amount of artificiality in the use of 's. I can testify from personal experience that copy editors have a habit of changing bare NPs to NPs with 's, so that such questions as 'house style' tend to come into it as well.

The length of NPs remains relevant in -ing constructions: it seems quite simply that long NPs, especially those with postnominal modifiers, avoid 's. The precise construction in which those NPs are embedded seems irrelevant. The role of definiteness seems rather tenuous in normal NPs; it is even more so in -ing forms. Emphasis, however, does seem to be relevant, at least as far as I can decide; compare the following forms:

57. a. I don't mind if you come, but I object to MARY coming
    b. ?I don't mind if you come, but I object to MARY's coming

One further point relates to the differentiation of subjects and objects in action nominal constructions (in gerunds, of course, they are differentiated in roughly the same way as in sentences). With simple intransitive verbs, action nominals seem to obey the same sorts of criteria as simple possessive NPs:

58. a. the coming of war
    b. *war's coming
    c. *the coming of him
    d. his coming

But with transitive verbs, as we have seen, there is a strong tendency for (active) subjects to precede and objects to follow, even when only one NP appears:

59. a. John's killing   (John is agent)
    b. The killing of John   (John is patient)

Even in famous 'ambiguous' examples like the shooting of the hunters, this tendency appears in terms of a marked preference for the object reading. But inanimate NPs still avoid 's, so that a subject reading with inanimate NPs may be simply inexpressible with an action nominal:

60. a. *Deadly nightshade's killing
    b. The killing of deadly nightshade (with weedkiller)

All of the factors mentioned so far relate to the internal syntax of the gerundive construction. There are also factors external to the gerundive construction which favour one or the other variant.

An obvious example of this is the construction with
<u>without</u>:
> 61. They moved it without him (*his) being
> notified

This pattern seems to work with other prepositions
as well:
> 62. a. I am against him (*his) being moved
> b. Instead of him (*his) coming here, we
> went there
> c. With him (*his) supporting us we can't go
> wrong

This also covers cases where the preposition <u>of</u>
follows an abstract noun:
> 63. The mere thought of me (*my) marrying her is
> preposterous

Of course, not all prepositions show this pattern:
temporal prepositions hardly ever occur with
subjectful gerunds:
> 64. *After him/his coming to see us, we left
> hurriedly

The verb which governs a gerundive construction may
also be selective as to which form it allows:
> 65. We saw him (*his) working
> 66. We saw his (*him) working as a threat to
> union solidarity

In all of these cases a major motivation of
these restrictions can be seen as semantic. The
possessive-gerund construction is typically used to
refer to states of affairs which are considered
facts; the 'accusative-gerund' construction is not
restricted in this way. Indeed in some typically
'factive' environments, the accusative-gerund is odd
or unacceptable:
> 67. a. I thoroughly regret my (*me) being
> involved in that
> b. The fact of my (*me) being here was
> remarked upon

We might hypothesise that the 'accusative-gerund'
construction represents the 'bare proposition',
while the possessive-gerund represents that same
proposition as a fact. Contrast the following pair,
for instance:
> 68. a. Me eating snails? You must be joking!
> b. My eating snails? You must be joking!

(68a) casts doubt on the suggestion that I eat/have
eaten snails - i.e. on its factual status. (68b), on
the other hand, cannot be interpreted in this way.
It requires a context in which the **fact** of my eating
snails is interpreted in a particular way - e.g. if
someone has said that the fact that I eat snails is
evidence of a luxurious way of life ('You must be

joking; I can only afford to eat them because my garden is full of them').

I think that there is something to be said for an approach of this sort. There is at least one problem, though. It hardly does justice to the uses of the accusative-gerund construction to say that it expresses a bare proposition; e.g. you can't see a bare proposition any more than you can see a fact, and yet this construction occurs in the complement of <u>see</u>. Nor is it sufficient to say that this construction takes on all possible meanings, because it does not - e.g. it does not occur in environments characteristic of manner phrases:

69. *Him doing that was rather inefficient

We seem to be left merely with a contrast of factivity.

EXERCISE 3

Look at as many spontaneous instances of subjectful gerunds as you can. (Of necessity these will probably occur in formal English rather than in informal conversation.) Does the factivity contrast account for all cases of the possessive-non-possessive contrast? Are there any further factors which seem relevant?

8.5. THE STRUCTURE OF GERUND AND ACTION NOMINALS

So far I have looked at a variety of aspects of the behaviour of gerundive and action nominal constructions, but without going in much detail into the question of the syntactic structure of these constructions. With action nominals it seems reasonably clear that they have a structure rather like those of other noun phrases: in particular, the action nominal is a head noun, the 'subject' is a normal possessive premodifier, and the 'object' is a normal prepositional phrase postmodifier. Thus the structure of an action nominal such as:

70. John's reading of books

is not essentially different from that of a normal NP like:

71. John's aunt from Maidenhead

This cannot be related to a sentence of the form:

72. John V-ed from Maidenhead

It is therefore to be assumed that the meaning of a normal NP such as (71) follows from the relationships of the various constituents, as marked by the possessive morpheme and preposition. The same could therefore be true of the action nominal (70). Its relationship with the sentence

73. John reads books

then follows simply from the fact that each of them contains the same elements, and each of them contains devices for marking similar relationships between these elements. All of the variant structures which make up action nominals have parallels in ordinary noun phrases; there is no good reason for suggesting that action nominals are other than ordinary noun phrases.

The case of the gerund is rather less straightforward, and there has been much disagreement in the literature. There is a certain convenient looseness in the term 'nominal'. In principle it is the adjective derived from the term 'noun', but in practice it is also used to refer to things which have the property of noun **phrases.** There is no doubt, for instance, that gerundive expressions are noun phrases: they occur in all of the positions characteristic of noun phrases - most typically subject position, object position, and as complement of a preposition:

74. a. John's mending his bicycle is astounding
     b. I appreciated John's mending my bicycle
     c. Because of John's mending my bicycle, I
        cycled in to work

In that sense, therefore, the gerundive expression is clearly 'nominal'. However, the looseness of the term carries with it the danger that it will be assumed that the gerund - i.e. the verb stem + ing - is itself a **noun.** I imagine that the list of properties mentioned in section 8.1 should be sufficient to dispel this illusion. The gerund does not behave in any way like a noun, except for the fact that it occurs within a noun phrase and is preceded (sometimes) by a possessive-marked NP. The action nominal, by contrast, has all the standard features which we might expect a noun to have - it co-occurs with articles and adjectives, it has no verbal features such as aspectual markers or adverbs, and the prepositional marking of its 'objects' is formally no different from the sorts of prepositional complement that any noun is capable of occurring with.

While there is not much merit in the suggestion that gerunds are nouns, an intermediate position has been suggested by Schachter. In this account, the gerundive construction consists of a determiner (which may be null, as in ordinary NPs) and a 'NOM',

which is a VP. One can compare the more traditional
account of gerunds as non-finite sentences (schemat-
ically represented in (75a)) with Schachter's proposal (75b), and with the generally accepted acount
for action nominals (75c):

75. a.

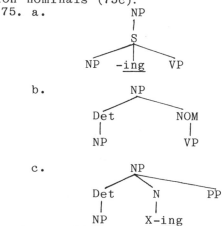

Schachter bases his argument on a wide range of
points - the determiner-like nature of the elements
which precede the gerund, the non-occurrence of
certain sentence-like properties in the gerundive
construction, the differing distribution of gerundive constructions and other sentence-like constituents, etc. It is not appropriate here to embark on a
critique of Schachter's proposal. However, some of
the points which he makes raise interesting general
questions.

His argument around determiners, for instance,
is a good example of the problems of describing
things which only partially fit into a pattern. In
saying that the genitive NP position before gerunds
is a determiner position, he is committed to the
possibility of other determiners occurring there,
e.g.

76. a. I won't tolerate any more telling tales
    b. This rewriting history has to stop

These are tolerably acceptable sentences, although
some people find them rather marginal. So Schachter
says that the position is a determiner position. But
then we predict the possibility of:

77. a. *I fancy some eating peanuts
    b. *It involved too much writing letters

Now it is certainly not the case that all determiners can occur in all positions; cases such as the
incompatibility of the indefinite article and
abstract or mass nouns (*a justice, *a sand) are

evidence of that. But such cases are not merely idiosyncratic instances; they fall under a regularity which can be easily stated (as I have just done). If the pre-gerund position is a determiner, then it needs to be argued what range of determiners can occur there.

Another point which seems to give rise to complications is the similarity of the gerundive construction to a sentence. Schachter points out that initial adverbials do not occur in gerundive constructions; in this they are like NPs, but not like sentences:

78. a. Perhaps I was mistaken
   b. *I acknowledge perhaps my having been mistaken (with <u>perhaps</u> relating to the gerund!)
   c. *The fact of perhaps my mistake was sufficient

But certain other tests seem to point to gerunds being just like sentences and not like NPs. Thus, the use of postposed <u>either</u> is characteristic of sentences and gerunds, but not of action nominals:

79. a. I missed the target and John didn't hit it either
   b. They laughed at my missing the target and John's not hitting it either
   c. *They laughed at my missing of the target, and John's not (non-?) hitting of it either

A further point here is that it is generally agreed that adverb such as <u>perhaps</u>, <u>unfortunately</u>, etc. relate to sentences and not just to verb phrases. The fact that these occur with gerundive constructions (albeit not initially) would argue for the sentential status of gerundive constructions:

80. Some people were amused at his unfortunately being omitted

I confess to not being convinced by Schachter's arguments. The very notion of a NOM constituent seems quite <u>ad</u> <u>hoc</u> to me. I would prefer the more traditional position that gerundive constructions are non-finite sentences. Personal preferences apart, it has to be admitted that there are many phenomena which are unexplained on any account. In my view, the value of presenting different suggestions as to syntactic structure is that one can then develop systematically different predictions from the different approaches. Preliminary formulation of such predictions provides a useful framework for discovering new facts about particular constructions, and, perhaps more importantly, for evaluating the significance of facts which are already known about the construction under study.

EXERCISE 4

Follow this argument through a little more systematically. We have two competing hypotheses; one that gerunds are sentences, the other that they consist of a (usually possessive) determiner and a 'NOM' which is a verb phrase. What systematic differences would we expect given these two approaches? Is there solid evidence for or against either of these approaches?

READING - CHAPTER 8

There's a lot of literature on this particular problem, but not a lot of it is very enlightening. An exception is the article by Schachter 'A nontransformational account of gerundive nominals in English' Linguistic Inquiry 7. Chomsky's still much-referred-to article 'Remarks on nominalisation' in Jacobs & Rosenbaum (eds) Readings in English Transformational Grammar is not an easy read, and the points made in it are of greater value for their criticism of others than for the positive proposals put forward. T. Wasow and T. Roeper 'On the subject of gerunds' Foundations of Language 8, 1972 is one of a number of articles distinguishing basically nominal -ing forms (the 'action nominal') from basically verbal ones (the gerund). There is a large literature on the possibility of occurrence of two -ings together, see for instance D. Bolinger 'The jingle theory of double -ing', in D. Allerton, R. Carney and D. Holdcroft (eds) Function and Context in Linguistic Analysis, Cambridge, 1979, pp41-56.
   The standard grammars are also worth looking at, because they put a very wide variety of interpretations on verb forms in -ing.

Chapter Nine

NON-FINITE SENTENCE COMPLEMENTS

In the last chapter we looked at the gerund in the
light of its relationship to the action nominal. In
this chapter and the next, I shall be illustrating
some of the problems which arise on looking at
gerundive, infinitive and finite subordinate sentences from the point of view of their occurrence as
subjects or (especially) objects of verbs - i.e. as
sentence complements. The sort of problem which
crops up in the case of non-finite complements can
be illustrated with the following sentences, where
the gerund and the infinitive have different
privileges of occurrence, and different semantic
effects:

    1. a. I want to come
       b. *I want coming
    2. a. *He enjoyed to hunt
       b. He enjoyed hunting
    3. a. He wants to shoot
       b. He wants shooting
    4. a. He began to shoot
       b. He began shooting
    5. a. He stopped to shoot
       b. He stopped shooting

Here we have cases where only one or the other form
is possible, a case where both forms occur with
apparently the same meaning (i.e. (4)), and cases
where both forms occur, but with completely different meanings. The complement of (3a) differs from
that of (3b) in meaning just as an active sentence
differs from a passive. (Of course, the meaning of
want is also rather different.) In (5), on the other
hand, it is the same person doing the shooting in
both cases, but (5a) is understood as a purpose
clause ('in order to shoot'), and would not generally be regarded as a real sentence complement (i.e.
it is not the object of the verb stop), while in

(5b) the gerund is interpreted as the thing that is stopped.

There is a very large set of verbs which take infinitive and/or gerundive complements, and it is the basis for the difference between these types of complement that I want to look at here. Of course it is possible to give a fairly basic account of the difference by simply marking verbs as being the sort which occur with the gerund, the sort which occur with the infinitive, or the sorts which occur with both or neither. But this would effectively mean a renunciation of any attempt to find a general basis for the distinction, and, as we shall see, there are certainly properties with a certain degree of generality which differentiate these constructions. However, before looking for such properties, it is as well to make a few preliminary distinctions.

One of the distinctions which is most crucial is that between subject and object complements. It has often been observed that the relationship between a verb and its object is very much closer and more constrained than that between a verb and its subject - i.e. verbs generally impose constraints on the form that their complements take; we have already looked at prepositional verbs in previous chapters. But parallel constraints on the form of subjects do not occur. In the area of sentence complements, the major manifestation of this difference is the much tighter nature of the constraints imposed by the verb on the form and nature of its object than on the subject. Of course, and as we shall see in rather more detail soon, there are semantic constraints on the complements of individual verbs - both subject and object - which will tend to be observed irrespective of syntactic position. But insofar as there are (apparently) purely formal constraints on the nature of the complement, these are much more noticeable with objects than with subjects. Contrast the data of (1)-(5) with examples such as:

6. a. That John came is rather odd
   b. John's having come is rather odd
   c. For John to have come would be rather odd

(We shall come back to cases such as (6c) and the reasons for the change in modality in the main clause.) There is a sense, therefore, in which the impossibility of a subject complement of a particular form will tell us something about the semantic factors which constrain the occurrence of complements, while the possibility or otherwise of object complements will depend on a rather greater variety of factors.

A further factor which needs to be taken into account is the range of infinitive complements which occur. The full form of the infinitive complement consists of the complementiser <u>for</u>, a subject NP, <u>to</u> and a verb phrase. This full form is extremely rare in object complements (more so in what I take to be standard British English than in at least some forms of American English). The reduced form of the infinitive complement lacks the <u>for</u> and the NP of the full form. But infinitive clauses are of two distinct types: consider a contrast such as that between (7a) and (7b):

7. a. Denis persuaded Maggie to retire
   b. Denis expected Maggie to retire

These two sentences have identical general form, yet they differ in certain crucial ways. (7b) could be a response to (8b), but there is no (8a) for (7a) to be a response to:

8. a. *What did Denis persuade?
   b. What did Denis expect

(7a) and (7b) have different types of paraphrase with finite complements:

9. a. Denis persuaded Maggie that she should retire
   b. Denis expected that Maggie would retire

Various other sentence types demonstrate that <u>Maggie</u> in (7a) is the 'real' object of <u>persuade</u>, but that the whole sentence complement is the object of <u>expect</u>:

10. a. *John persuaded advantage to be taken of the situation
    b. John expected advantage to be taken of the situation

11. a. *John persuaded it to rain
    b. John expected it to rain

Differences of this sort led transformational grammarians to claim that sentences like (7a) should be related to structures like that of (9a), with a general **deletion** rule disposing of the 'excess' NP (<u>she</u>) if it is identical in reference to some other NP (here <u>Maggie</u>). (7b), by contrast, is analysed as being related to a structure like (9b) by a **movement** rule - from embedded subject position to matrix object position. More recently an alternative analysis has been put forward, which differs from the transformational one in claiming that <u>Maggie</u> in (7b) is not the object of <u>expect</u> at all, underlyingly or superficially, but only the subject of <u>retire</u>. The differences between these accounts, though far-reaching, should not obscure the fact that they specify the same distinctions of structure. From the perspective of this chapter, it is more natural to adopt the traditional transformational approach - partly on the terminological grounds that it provides convenient labels ('deletion', 'movement') for the two types, and partly on the (contentious) grounds that, when couched in these terms, it is generalisable to a distinction of a slightly different sort:

12. a. Maggie is eager to retire
    b. Maggie is likely to retire

Sentences directly analogous to (8)-(11) back up this distinction:

13. a. *What is eager?
    b. What is likely?
14. a. Maggie is eager that she should retire
    b. That Maggie will retire is likely
15. a. *Advantage is eager to be taken of the situation
    b. Advantage is likely to be taken of the situation
16. a. *It is eager to rain
    b. It is likely to rain

The difference between (7) and (12) is that (7) is a contrast of a three-place verb (persuade) and a two-place verb (expect), while (12) is a contrast between a two-place adjective (eager) and a one-place adjective (likely). Otherwise there are clear parallels. So we can say that (12a) is a deletion structure, while (12b) is a movement structure. Of course this is not intended to preclude non-transformational formulations; but the transformational analysis provides handy labels to fit on these constructions.

9.2. SOME HYPOTHESES ABOUT NON-FINITE COMPLEMENTS

There are several hypotheses which have been put forward, both on a syntactic and a semantic basis, to account for different types of non-finite sentence complements. The following is a sample of some of the things that have been said in this area:

A. Infinitives have been seen as resulting uniquely from grammatical processes (i.e. the deletion and movement processes of the last section) which result in the absence of a subject noun phrase; in other words, any sentence which for any reason emerges lacking a subject is in the infinitive form.

B. Gerunds are often said to be typically

'factive'; - i.e. they express a proposition whose truth is presupposed within the sentence.

C. Infinitives are sometimes also seen as representing an 'unrealised' or 'irrealis' mood; i.e. the events or states referred to in infinitive sentences have not actually happened at the time of speaking, but are represented as hypothetical, or as occurring in the future.

D. It is sometimes noted that the gerund-infinitive distinction is formally similar to the distinction between progressive and non-progressive aspect, and it might be claimed that the semantic distinction between the forms is similar.

I have chosen these hypotheses because they all appear to have some truth in them; at the same time it would be surprising if they were entirely adequate. I am saved from the task of compiling lists of relevant verbs, because this has already been done (in an Indiana University project). Some of the relevant tables are appended (Tables 9.1-5 at the end of the chapter), although there are many other tables which could be relevant in addition. We can use these tables for preliminary evaluation of the hypotheses (A)-(D).

All of (A) - (D) fall down in one way or another: (A) appears to suggest that there ought to be no infinitives with subjects. But, as we have seen, infinitives do occur with subjects, as in (17):

17. For John to say that is contemptible

Furthermore, there are uses of the infinitive where there is no evidence that a subject has been moved or deleted in the ways we saw above:

18. a. It is odd to say that
    b. To err is human

And of course gerunds can also be considered to be complement sentences lacking subjects (in some cases); the nature of the difference would need to be further elaborated on. So although (A) might make a reasonably adequate account of many infinitive structures, it cannot account for them all. There is also the point that this proposal is heavily dependent on a particular theoretical framework; there is nothing wrong in this, of course, but it does mean that the evaluation of such a proposal is inseparable from the evaluation of the overall theoretical framework - a task which goes beyond the goals of this book.

(B) is also valid only within limits. Acknowledge, admit, appreciate, etc. are examples where the analysis works: (19) can only be true (or false) if he really was showered with fivers:

19. John appreciated being showered with fivers

But a glance at the list (Table 9.1) shows that there are many verbs which take gerundive complements which involve no such presupposition - e.g. <u>consider</u>, <u>contemplate</u>, <u>debate</u>, <u>imagine</u>, <u>intend</u>. As well as being apparent counterexamples to (B), these verbs also appear to be counterexamples to (C) as, apart from <u>intend</u>, they all fail to take infinitive complements, and yet they all suggest that the action or state specified in the complement is either projected into the future or unreal in some other way (as with <u>imagine</u>). We therefore fail to get the expected:

20. a. *John is contemplating to emigrate
    b. *I imagine to have been the first person
       to say this

Of course, some of these verbs (<u>consider</u>, <u>imagine</u>, <u>intend</u>) do take an infinitive complement with a <u>moved</u> subject, if not with a deleted one (cf. section 9.1):

21. a. I consider him to be clever
    b. I intend this to be a brilliant chapter

We shall return to these shortly. (C) also faces problems from verbs such as <u>contrive</u> and <u>manage</u>:

22. He managed to open the door

Managing (or contriving) to do something entails doing that thing, and therefore there is no sense in which the infinitive complement in (22) can be said to be 'unreal' or 'unrealised'. The number of exceptions such as this does not appear to be large, but nevertheless, they suggest that (C) is untenable as a hypothesis about all infinitives.

(D) also, I think, has some truth in it - the best illustration being <u>see</u>:

23. a. I saw him coming
    b. I saw him come
    c. He was seen to come

The infinitive complement lacks a <u>to</u> in the active form, but has one in the passive. The reference of (23b) is to a completed action - it was his arrival that I saw - while (23a) refers to an action in progress. However, there are problems for (D) in that an overt progressive-non-progressive distinction is made even within simple infinitive complements:

24. a. I want to win
    b. I want to be winning when he comes
    c. *I want winning when he comes

If the progressive meaning of gerunds were a regular part of English grammar, then (24b) would be unnecessary, and (24c) would be used in its place. (Of

course (24c) might be considered marginally acceptable if I were a prize.)
   As all of the general hypotheses mentioned here
face serious problems, there are two natural steps
which seem worth considering. The first is to move
on to consider further hypotheses, the problem of
course being to decide what these might reasonably
be. The other possibility is to break down the
different types of complement into subclasses, and
provide further refinement of the subclassification
of verbs, in the hope that some of the hypotheses
already considered might actually work on a definable subset of the broad classification already
arrived at. It is rather easier to find natural
subclasses of infinitive complements, so in what
follows I shall try to provide an outline of a more
detailed classification of infinitives.
   I have already referred (in section 9.1) to the
distinction between deletion and movement in
infinitive complements. This imposes a three-way
classification on verbs which occur with infinitive
complements in object position. Some verbs allow
only complements with deleted subjects - i.e. their
infinitive complements can only be understood as
having the same subject as the main verb - e.g.
attempt, begin, condescend, continue, fail, manage,
proceed, refuse, start and try. Other verbs allow
only complements with moved subjects - e.g. fancy,
presume, prove (in its evidential sense), require,
think. The third group of verbs allows both possibilities - e.g. expect, fear, hate, intend, like,
mean, need, prefer, want. The difference can be
illustrated with the behaviour of a representative
member of each group:
   25. a. I managed to open the door
       b. *I managed him to open the door
   26. a. *I presumed to have got lost
       b. I presumed him to have got lost
(Presume occurs in structures like (26a) with the
meaning 'dare', but I presume that this is a
distinct verb.)
   27. a. I expect to get out soon
       b. I expect him to get out soon
A further group of verbs with infinitive complements
consists of those verbs which have subjectless complements (derived by deletion) and a NP object which
is interpreted as being the subject of the complement sentence. For this group, see the examples and
discussion in section 9.1. Further examples are
admonish, advise, challenge, force, etc.
   These four groups of verbs are mutually exclus-

ive in that, although some of their members may occur in more than one group because of having different meanings, a single verb with a single meaning will occur only in one of these groups. However, it is also possible to subdivide verbs taking infinitive complements in a way which does not coincide with this classification. For instance, many verbs allow 'full' infinitive complements as objects (i.e. complements of the form 'for NP to VP'), and also have deleted-subject infinitive complements, and simple NP objects preceded by the preposition for. This class includes verbs such as arrange, aim, aspire, beg, bid, hope, itch, labour, long, opt, etc.:

28. a. I arranged for him to come
    b. I arranged to come
    c. I arranged for a babysitter

Note that the association of the preposition for and the infinitive complement is not merely restricted to this type of construction. Clauses of purpose also occur in the infinitive construction, and purpose phrases typically begin with for:

29. a. I went away to get a rest
    b. I went away for a rest

The classes delimited by these criteria are already more homogeneous. The infinitive-taking verbs which could not count as 'irrealis' are all in the class of deletion-only verbs: we could hypothesise that C applies to movement infinitives only. The for-complement verbs just mentioned also seem semantically quite homogeneous: the complement sentence describes a situation for which the matrix subject is aiming. Other subclasses are possible: Tables 9.2 and 9.3 illustrate the fact that certain verbs allow only a small set of main verbs in infinitive complements, while others are less restricted. The restriction on the verbs in 9.2 seems to be largely that they should be stative:

30. a. I believe her to hate knitting
    b. ??I believe her to hit John

But a **generic** interpretation of an active verb is quite possible:

31. I believe her to beat her children

However, a careful look at the verbs in Table 9.2 shows that there is considerable variation in the types of complement which they allow (and perhaps also considerable variation among speakers).

EXERCISE 1

Apply this rather more refined classification to the data of Tables 9.2 and 9.3 Are the results any more satisfactory or homogeneous than they were with a cruder classification?

9.3. 'MINIMAL PAIRS' WITH GERUND AND INFINITIVE

Another way of approaching the difference between gerundive and infinitival complements is to confront them in situations where both can occur naturally. Tables 9.1 and 9.4 give over thirty pairs of this type, e.g. begin, continue, fear, hate, intend, like, prefer, propose, remember, start and try. The situation is made more complex by the fact that there are other verbs which are in some ways similar in meaning to some of these, but which do not allow the same flexibility of complements. E.g. enjoy is similar to like, but does not allow infinitive complements; recall is like remember, and equally does not allow infinitive complements; keep on is similarly restricted, although it means something like continue, as does resume. I shall look at each of these cases in turn.

Enjoy and like are certainly similar in some ways, but enjoy is more restricted in that it cannot refer to anything which is not a process currently happening. Cf. for instance:
32. a. I would like to come tomorrow
    b. I would enjoy coming tomorrow
(32b) suggests a projection of the enjoyment - i.e. when I come tomorrow, I will enjoy it. (32a) does not altogether suggest that I shall like the experience of coming tomorrow when it happens. It may be that the event planned for tomorrow is a highly instructive, but at the same time highly unpleasant experience, and that the speaker of (32a) feels that it would be highly useful to go along, even though he is sure that he will not actually like the experience. (32a), but not (32b), could have the added clause 'though I'm sure I'll hate every minute of it' without being made nonsensical. What one enjoys is the experience; what one likes (when it is used with the infinitive) is the prospect, or the generalised idea of the activity. I think that it is exactly the same distinction which is made between the two different complements of like:
33. a. I like to eat 3 lbs. of raw meat before

training sessions
b. I like eating 3 lbs. of raw meat before training sessions

(33a) suggests that the speaker eats the meat because he thinks it is good for him, while (33b) suggests that he does it because it makes him feel good doing it, because he likes the experience.

The difference between <u>recall</u> and <u>remember</u> is quite simple. You recall events from the past, but remembering involves bringing anything up from memory, including the need to do certain things. Where <u>remember</u> is used interchangeably with <u>recall</u>, it can only take a gerund as complement:

34. a. I recall paying tenpence for a pint of beer
b. I remember paying tenpence for a pint of beer

However, where the content of the complement is not what is brought up from memory, but the action which follows from bringing up some instruction from memory, then only the infinitive complement is possible:

35. I remembered to pay for the beer

The distinction between <u>continue</u> and <u>keep on</u> is not a relevant one in this context, as <u>keep on</u> ends in a preposition, and prepositions never govern infinitive complements. There is a semantic distinction between the two uses of <u>continue</u>, however, roughly along the lines that the gerundive version refers to a continuation of the same process, while the infinitive version refers to another, or several other, processes of the same sort - other tokens of the same type. This can be illustrated with some rather tentative judgements on data such as the following:

36. a. After his first chapter had been rejected by the publishers, he continued writing the book
b. ?After his first chapter had been rejected by the publisher he continued to write the book

37. a. After his first book had been rejected by the publishers, he continued to write books that were never published
b. ??After his first book had been rejected by the publishers, he continued writing books that were never published

These judgements, especially that on (36b), are tentative in the extreme. <u>Kept on writing</u> would be fully acceptable in either of these contexts. The same distinction as this can be made with other 'phasal' verbs - i.e. verbs which refer to beginnings, middles and ends of situations:

38. a. The Queen started collapsing
    b. The Queen started to collapse

Both of the sentences in (38) are compatible with an iterative interpretation - i.e. she developed a tendency to collapse, and had already done so a few times. There is another possible interpretation which refers to a particular occasion, an interpretation which would be forced if we continued 'but was supported by her entourage'. This interpretation is much more natural with (38b) than it is with (38a).

If you look very carefully at this contrast, you will find that there is an apparent contradiction here. With <u>continue</u>, if my judgements are accepted, it is the gerund which is favoured when a single event is at issue, while with <u>start</u> it is the infinitive. I suspect that this contrast is only apparent; if we look on the gerund as being possible usually when the 'actuality' or 'reality' of the action is evident, then it follows that the gerund will not be used where the action has not actually happened. In an iterative interpretation of (38), the Queen actually has collapsed a few times, and therefore we can look on the action as being 'real'. But if, at a given time, she is only just starting to collapse, then the collapsing is not fully truc - she has not collapsed. But if one continues to write, this can only be true if one has already done some writing , and there is therefore a basis of 'real' action to support the use of the gerund. This suggestion is rather a vague one (can you do better?), but it seems to me to bear at least some relation to what is likely to be the 'real' explanation.

In the light (or dark) of this set of data, it would appear that there is some considerable truth in an approach to the gerundive complement as expressing 'factuality' or 'actuality'. Insofar as my judgements are clear on the other cases mentioned, it would appear that these too support the same distinction. E.g. <u>try</u> (which might reasonably be considered to represent two entirely different verbs) is used with the gerund when it refers to a successful action which the subject intends to evaluate, while it is used with the infinitive when it is referring to an action which is not necessarily successful:

39. a. John tried using a bigger bar of soap
    b. John tried to open the door

EXERCISE 2

Find more examples of the alternation of gerundive and infinitival complements and contrast them in a similar way. Do they fit in with the sorts of considerations put forward here?

READING - CHAPTER 9

The tables are taken from D. Alexander & W. J. Kunz Some classes of verbs in English and L. I. Bridgeman et al. More classes of verbs in English, both produced in connection with the Linguistics Research Project at Indiana University (Principal Investigator F. W. Householder Jr, Assistant Director P. H. Matthews) and made available by Indiana University Linguistics Club. The notion of factivity was introduced by P and C.Kiparsky 'Fact', M. Bierwisch and K. Heidolph (eds) Progress in Linguistics, The Hague: Mouton, 1970. There is a very large transformational literature on such complement structures, most of which will tell you a lot about transformational grammar, but not very much about the questions considered here. A good general survey of relatively early work is R. Stockwell, P. Schachter & B. Partee The Major Syntactic Structures of English (Holt), while if you want to look in detail at how late standard transformational grammar would deal with this, refer to P. Postal On Raising: One Rule of English Grammar and its Theoretical Implications (MIT). The more recent 'Government and Binding' approach is perhaps best introduced by A. Radford Transformational Syntax, Cambridge, 1981.

Non-finite sentence complements

Table 9.1. Verbs occurring in the context
NP ＿＿ Gerund

abide		discuss		*profess	a
accept	a	*disdain		propose	
acknowledge		dislike		protest	a
adore		doubt	a	query	a
adduce		dread		question	a
admit		dream of		rate	
affect	a	*endure		recall	
afford		enjoy		*recollect	
*announce		envisage		refrain from	
anticipate		escape	a	register	a
appreciate		evade		regret	
attempt		explain		relate	a
avoid		fancy		relish	
bear		favour		remember	
*bear in mind		fear		*repent	a
begin		*feign		report	
*blame	a	finish		*repudiate	a
bother		forbear		*request	a
brook		foresee		*require	a
call to mind	a	forget		resent	a
can help		go on		*suffer	a
can stand		hate		suggest	
cease		*ignore	a	take	
chance		imagine		*take to	
*choose		insist on		*threaten	
commence		intend		tolerate	
comprehend	a	keep		*treasure	
*conceive	a	keep from		trouble	
*confess		*lament		try	
*confirm		like		*underline	a
consider		loathe		*understand	
contemplate		love		*undertake	
continue		*manage		resist	
count on		mention		reveal	a
debate		mind		risk	
*decline		miss		save	a
deliberate		omit		scorn	
deny		plan on		*scruple	
describe	a	plead	a	*see	
deserve		practice		*stand	a
disclaim	a	practise		start	
*disclose	a	*predict		stop	
discontinue		prefer			

'*' indicates a dubious case for inclusion
'a' indicates that the complement is best if it
starts with <u>have</u>, <u>be</u>, <u>want</u>, <u>need</u>, etc.

Table 9.2. Verbs occurring in the contexts
          NP ___ NP to VP
     or   NP be ___ -ed to VP

acknowledge	declare	*glean	quote
adjudge	decree	grant	read
admit	deduce	guarantee	realise
advertise	deem	guess	*reason
affirm	define	hear	recall
allege	demonstrate	hint	reckon
allow	deny	hold	recognise
*analyse	depict	hypothesise	recollect
announce	describe	imagine	record
apprehend	descry	indicate	recount
*argue	detect	*infer	register
ascertain	determine	interpret	remember
*assert	discern	intuit	report
assume	disclose	judge	represent
*aver	discover	know	repute
*avouch	display	learn	reveal
bear	*distinguish	make out	rule
believe	divine	maintain	see
*betray	*divulge	*measure	sense
*boast	doubt	*mention	show
calculate	*dream	mistake	signify
can stand	envisage	*misunderstand	specify
certify	*espy	note	state
*cite	establish	opine	stipulate
*claim	esteem	overhear	suppose
*comprehend	estimate	own	surmise
*compute	*exhibit	perceive	suspect
concede	explain	point out	swear
conceive	fancy	posit	take
*conclude	fear	postulate	*testify
confess	feel	presume	think
confirm	figure	presuppose	understand
*conjecture	find	proclaim	*uphold
consider	foresee	profess	verify
construe	*foretell	pronounce	wager
*contend	give	prophesy	warrant
*count	give out	prove	witness

The verbs in this table are restricted to occurring
with complements beginning be, have, etc.

Table 9.3. Verbs which occur without restriction in
the contexts   NP ___ NP to VP
                      NP be ___ -ed to VP

---

*accept	*design	inspire	qualify
adjure	designate	instruct	radio
admonish	desire	intend	raise
advise	destine	invite	rear
allow	determine	lead	recommend
appoint	direct	license	rehearse
ask	*discipline	like	remind
assign	disincline	*loathe	request
*assist	*dislike	love	require
authorise	dispose	*march	resolve
badger	doom	mean	retain
beckon	drill	motion	rush
beg	drive	motivate	say
*behold	*dun	move	secure
*beseech	embolden	nag	see
*bid	elect	name	select
bind	employ	need	send
*bother	empower	nominate	sentence
bribe	enable	*notice	signal
*bring	encourage	notify	slate
cable	engage	oblige	solicit
*call	enjoin	observe	spur on
cause	entice	*ordain	*start
caution	entitle	order	stimulate
challenge	entreat	pay	sue
charge	exhort	permit	suffer
choose	expect	persuade	summon
*coach	favour	pester	teach
*coax	figure	petition	telephone
*coerce	forbid	'phone	*telegraph
command	force	phone	tell
commission	*forewarn	pick	tempt
compel	get	plead with	*tolerate
condemn	*goad	pledge	train
condition	hate	predestine	trouble
constrain	help	predetermine	trust
*contract	hire	predict	tutor
convince	*hound	predispose	urge
counsel	*hurry	prefer	want
count on	impel	press	warn
dare	implore	prevail upon	will
*decide	importune	*prod	wire
delegate	incite	prompt	wish
deploy	incline	provoke	write
depute	induce	*push	

161

Non-finite sentence complements

Table 9.4. Verbs occurring in the context
NP ___ <u>to</u> VP

---

*ache	decline	like	qualify
affect	deign	*loathe	refuse
afford	demand	long	*regret
agree	deserve	look	remain
aim	desire	love	remember
appear	determine	*make	*repent
arrange	*dislike	manage	require
ask	*discontinue	mean	resolve
aspire	disdain	*mention	*say
*assay	*draw	*motion	scorn
assist	dread	move	scruple
attempt	elect	need	see fit
*avouch	endeavour	neglect	seek
avow	*endure	*negotiate	seem
bear	*essay	offer	*send
*beg	expect	omit	serve
begin	fail	opt	*shoot
*bid	*fancy	*ordain	stand
bother	fear	*persist	start
*brook	*figure	*pine	strive
*buck	*fix	plan	suffice
can stand	forbear	*plead	swear
care	forget	pledge	tend
cease	get	prefer	think
*champ	*go	prepare	threaten
chance	grow	presume	trouble
choose	happen	pretend	try
claim	hasten	proceed	turn out
come	hate	profess	undertake
commence	have	*proffer	venture
condescend	hesitate	promise	volunteer
consent	hope	propose	vote
continue	intend	*propound	*vouchsafe
contract	*itch	prove	vow
contrive	*know	*purpose	want
covenant	labor	*push	wish
dare	labour		yearn
decide	learn		

Table 9.5. Verbs occurring in the context
NP ___ for NP to VP

*ache	cry out	*message	ring
*add	decide	mind	say
afford	demand	motion	*see fit
agree	*direct	move	send
aim	*dislike	*mumble	*sign
answer	*emphasise	*need	signal
*appeal	*endeavour	*negotiate	*solicit
apply	entail	opt	specify
*argue	*entreat	petition	spell out
arrange	*fight	'phone	stipulate
ask	*gesture	phone	*stress
*bargain	hate	*pine	suggest
bear	hint	plan	*take care
beckon	*hope	plead	telephone
beg	*indicate	pray	telegraph
cable	*insinuate	*preach	time
call	intend	*prefer	*underline
can stand	*intimate	prepare	*undertake
*care	*itch	*prescribe	vote
check	*like	*press	wait
*choose	long	provide	watch
*consent	look	*push	*whisper
contract	*love	radio	wire
contrive	mean	recommend	*write
*cry	mention	*request	*yearn

Chapter Ten

FINITE SENTENCE COMPLEMENTS

In the last chapter we looked at non-finite sentence
complements, mainly those which occur in object
position. Of course, many of the verbs we looked at
also allow complements of other types, and there are
many other verbs which allow only finite complements. I shall leave this notion deliberately vague
- it would be natural to exclude subjunctive complements from the class of 'finite' clauses, for
instance - and shall use it in practice to refer to
complements which are neither infinitival nor
gerundive, and which are introduced either with that
or with a WH-word (interrogative sentence complements). Finite sentence complements are therefore
involved in the following sentences:
    1. a. I think that he is coming
       b. I suggest that he be examined again
       c. I asked who was going to come
There does not appear to be much doubt that simple
that-clauses are the 'neutral' pattern as far as
sentence complements are concerned: they are complements of more verbs, they have a wider range of
modal and tense/aspect possibilities than any other
type of sentence complement, and they probably
impose fewer semantic constraints on the verbs which
have them as complements. Nevertheless there are
verbs which do not allow that-clauses as complements. These seem to fall into two types: on the one
hand, the absence of finite complements seems to be
motivated in some natural way - verbs such as begin,
try, manage, etc. fail to accept finite complements
in many languages, and the interpretation of finite
complement clauses would probably pose problems even
if they were possible. The other group of verbs
seems to be restricted in a much more idiosyncratic
way, and other factors suggest that in principle
finite clauses ought to be possible with such verbs.

Finite sentence complements

Contrast the following three sentences which would
be equivalents in English, French and Russian, word-
for-word, if the English sentence were acceptable:
    2. a. *I want that he come
       b. Je veux qu'il vienne
       c. Ja xochu, chtoby on prishel
Cross-linguistic comparisons are suggestive but no
more. However, there is a certain amount of evidence
from within English that finite clauses are compatible with want, cf.:
    3. a. All I want is that he should come
       b. That he should come is what everybody
           wants
Some American speakers accept sentences such as:
    4. I want he should come
Interposition of an adverb between verb and complement makes for greater although, for me, by no means
complete acceptability:
    5. ??I want very much that he should come
All of these factors suggest that the major factor
contributing to the unacceptability of sentences
such as (2a) is the unacceptability of the simple
sequences want that. Similar restrictions are not
found with near-synonyms of want such as desire. It
may well be that the absence of a productive and
widely used subjunctive in English is relevant to
the peculiarity of want, given that analogous verbs
in other languages commonly require subjunctive
complements; it is nonetheless unlikely that there
can be any genuinely systematic account of the
unacceptability of finite complements with want.
    There is a very wide range of phenomena which
need to be clarified in the behaviour of finite
complements. I shall focus on just three topics
here. First, why is it that some verbs (want,
manage, etc.) occur only with non-finite complements
and other verbs (say, hope, etc.) occur with finite
complements? It is not necessary that there be an
answer to this question - it could be a matter of
arbitrary (or historically-determined) lexical
choices, but it is at least worth looking into the
question. Another issue is the occurrence of interrogative (as opposed to declarative) complements -
and of subjunctive complements, such as they are, as
well. We have distributions of these in various
permutations:
    6. a. I think that he came
       b. *I think that he come
       c. *I think whether he came
    7. a. I suggest that he came
       b. I suggest that he come

       c. *I suggest whether he came
8. a. *I asked that he came
    b. I asked that he come
    c. I asked whether he came
9. a. I'm not sure that he came
    b. *I'm not sure that he come
    c. I'm not sure whether he came

It can be seen from data such as these that there is no simple correspondence of verbs and individual complement types, and further data can easily be introduced which would further complicate the issue. It is therefore an interesting question whether any general basis for this choice of complement type is available. The third issue to be looked at is the question of when <u>that</u> can be omitted or not in finite complements. It is well-known that in some cases it cannot:

10. a. Everyone rejoiced that they won
    b. *Everyone rejoiced they won

Omission is seldom necessary, but it is more likely in some circumstances, less so in others. The details of this need to be looked at.

10.2. THE NON-OCCURRENCE OF FINITE COMPLEMENTS

As already mentioned, one of the salient aspects of simple <u>that</u>-clauses is the greater range of internal grammatical variation that they display in comparison with other types of complement. On the one hand they always have subject NPs, and on the other, a full range of tense-aspect marking and modal verb possibilities. Although there is a limited amount of tense-aspect variation allowed in non-finite clauses, the crucial fact here is that non-finite complements do not **require** any specification of tense or aspect; the simple infinitive form of the verb, or the simple gerundive form of the verb, is not to be interpreted as conveying a specific tense or aspect. This is not so with <u>that</u>-clauses, where the present tense has the same significance as in simple sentences (although with complications relating to 'sequence of tenses').

    Given this type of distinction, the various types of complement clause are obviously suited to the expression of different types of need. Contrast, for instance, <u>say</u> and <u>manage</u>. The sorts of things that people say can have reference to the past, the present, or some hypothetical or imaginary state; they can say things about themselves, or they can say things about other people or things. In other

words, the verb _say_ imposes no semantic constraints
either on the possible subject of its complement or
on the tense/aspect of its complement. _Manage_ is a
quite different case: it is what has been called an
'implicative' verb, meaning that if X manages to do
something, we can infer that he did it, while if X
does not manage to do something, we can infer that
he did not do it. The managing and the doing cannot
be separated temporally, nor can they be performed
by different people. Thus the sentences of (11) are
unacceptable:

    11. a. *John managed to have come
        b. *John managed for Bill to come

It is not difficult to see that if _manage_ were to be
followed by a finite complement, the degree of freedom allowed it would be totally wasted. Conversely,
if _say_ were not able to occur with _that_-clauses, the
sorts of things which can be said would simply not
be expressible in its complement. Most of the verbs
which occur only with non-finite complements are
like _manage_ in this respect, although some allow
slightly greater scope for tense-aspect variation:

    12. a. John tried to finish the work
        b. I shall try to have finished the work by
           the time you come

However, this added variability is constrained within very narrow limits, it being impossible to try to
do things in the past, for instance. Therefore the
limited range of variability which is allowed by the
infinitive is ample for the needs of a verb such as
try. Here a verb such as _want_ is the exception:
there is no semantic reason why you should not want
a situation to have occurred in the past, or something expressible with a modal such as _can_, _must_,
might, etc. It is just impossible with _want_, presumably an idiosyncratic fact about this verb, as is
suggested by its cross-linguistic patterning.

    There is a further interesting class of cases
where the finite clause cannot occur - after
prepositions. The only complement form which can
typically occur after a preposition is the gerund:

    13. a. *John was thinking about that he should
           come
        b. John was thinking about (Mary) coming

There is a pseudo-exception in the form of sentences
such as:

    14. His behaviour is appalling, in that he
        should never have broken his promise

But it really only makes sense to analyse _in that_ as
some sort of complex conjunction here, rather than a
combination of preposition and subordinate clause.

No other use of <u>in</u> can involve a following clause:
    15. a. *He is interested in that I came
        b. *I don't know why he believed in that I
           would come
Contrast the same frames with gerundive expressions
- e.g. <u>my coming</u>. However there are two ways in
which this incompatibility is manifested. After some
verbs and adjectives (and a few nouns as well) a
preposition must occur when there is a simple noun
phrase following, but when the string which occurs
is a finite sentence, the preposition is absent, and
obligatorily so (cf. (16)). Other verbs and adjectives which are followed by a preposition and a noun
phrase simply do not permit sentences to occur in
that position, with or without a preposition (cf.
(17)):
    16. a. Everyone was aware of it
          Everyone was aware that he was coming
        b. Everyone was surprised at it
          Everyone was surprised that he was coming
        c. I wouldn't bet on it
          I wouldn't bet that he is coming
        d. They persuaded her of it
          They persuaded her that he was coming
        e. He doesn't care about it
          He doesn't care that he is coming
        f. Everyone hopes for it
          Everyone hopes that he is coming
    17. a. John is relying on it
          *John is relying that he will come
        b. John is suffering from it
          *John is suffering that Bill hit him
        c. John talked about it
          *John talked that he was coming
        d. John thanked Bill for it
          *John thanked Bill that he was coming
        e. That was demonstrated by it
          *That was demonstrated that he was coming
        f. Everyone is ready for it
          *Everyone is ready that he is coming

EXERCISE 1

Extend the data of (16) and (17) by finding other
prepositional phrase contexts in which sentence
complements can or cannot occur. Do any general
bases emerge for the distinction between these two
types of behaviour?

10.3. INTERROGATIVE COMPLEMENT CLAUSES

There is one further point which deserves making in
relation to the choice of finite complement clause
with <u>that</u>. Until now I have tended to assume tacitly
in the discussion that the major factor distinguishing one type of complement from another is the
lexical and semantic properties of the complement-
taking verb. However, although this provides a
reasonable approximation to the truth for most
object complements, there are other syntactic
factors which are also relevant in determining the
nature of the complement type. One of the clearest
such cases involves negation, or interrogative formation in a main sentence, which frequently condition
a change of possible complement type:

18. a. John knows that he has a good chance
    b. *John knows whether he has a good chance
    c. John doesn't know that he has a good
       chance
    d. John doesn't know whether he has a good
       chance
    e. Does John know whether he has a good
       chance?

(I oversimplify slightly: (18b) is not too bad in a
contrastive use - i.e. where the question of people
knowing whether he has a good chance or not has
already been raised.)

19. a. John wonders whether she is angry
    b. *John wonders that she is angry
    c. Do you (ever) wonder whether she is
       angry?
    d. Do you wonder that she is angry?
    e. I don't wonder that she is angry

It seems likely that the data in (19) are accidental
- possibly deriving from the variant meanings of
<u>wonder</u> (involving 'musing' or 'wonderment'), with
varying degrees of archaicness. Other verbs which
select interrogative complements do not manifest the
same variation:

20. a. I asked whether he had come
    b. *I didn't ask that he had come

But the pattern illustrated in (18) is certainly not
accidental; many, though not all, of the verbs which
take <u>that</u>-complements also allow interrogative
complements when they are negated or questioned.
This gives us another dichotomous classification of
verbs, and another problem: what is the difference
between them? (21) is a list of verbs which behave
like <u>know</u> in (18), and (22) is a list of verbs which
occur with <u>that</u>-complements but do not alternate in

this way:
    21. announce, ascertain, check, confirm, consider, find out, remember, reveal, see, suggest, understand, etc.
    22. acknowledge, admit, agree, claim, expect, feel, persuade, regret, suppose, think, etc.
I.e. we get a pattern as in (23) and (24):
    23. a. She found out that he was a member
       b. Did she find out whether he was a member?
    24. a. I expect that he is a member
       b. *I don't expect whether he is a member

The question of why such a difference arises naturally leads on to the question of the nature of interrogative complements in general. The most straightforward account of interrogative complements is likely to be one in which all interrogative complements without exception are seen as expressing a single meaning or function, and in which, therefore, the nature of lists such as (21) and (22) follows from more general principles. What general differences could there be in such cases? A number of preliminary points seem necessary here.

- First, it is important to bear in mind the difference between (main clause) questions and requests; the semantic characteristics of a question are quite different from those of a request.

- Secondly, different syntactic distribution is found among interrogative complements beginning with whether or if and those beginning in some other way - this corresponds to the difference between yes-no questions and wh-questions in English.

- Thirdly, some embedded questions occur in a syntactic context which makes it clear that they are to be interpreted in roughly the same way as non-embedded questions (e.g. those following I wonder), while others clearly differ in import from main clause questions. Any general formulation will need to be neutral between these.

One obvious point of difference between embedded interrogatives with whether (I shall assume throughout that if can be subsumed here as well) and that-complements is that the interrogative clauses are concerned with the factual status of the proposition they contain, while that clauses can be highly variable in this respect. To take the most central type of interrogative, (25) below shows the subject of ask concerned with whether the embedded clause is true or not, while (26) with expect can have no such interpretation, simply by virtue of the nature of expectation:
    25. He asked whether there was any mail

26. He expected that there would be some mail

In main clause questions it is typically the case that the speaker does not know, or claims not to know, whether the proposition expressed in the question is true or not. In some embedded questions, the person that must be assumed not to know this information is the subject of the main clause (cf. 23), whereas for others it is the indirect object which fulfils this role - cf. (27)

27. He wouldn't reveal to us whether it was true

What seems to be relevant here is the fact that the relevant noun phrase represents the **Experiencer**, in case grammar terms - i.e. the participant in the sentence situation who is specified as registering (or not registering!) information. We can therefore formulate a condition on the possibility of embedded questions:

> The referent of the noun phrase occupying the Experiencer role in the main clause does not know if the proposition of the embedded clause is true, at the time specified by the tense of the main clause.

The nature of the difference between (21) and (22) then becomes rather clearer: e.g. given (28a) it is clear that this appropriateness condition is not fulfilled, but with the main verb in the negative, the condition is fulfilled:

28. a. *I remember whether he came
    b. I don't remember whether he came

With a verb like <u>regret</u>, on the other hand, it is clear that one can only regret something which has happened, so that this verb is only used in cases where the complement is true, therefore falling outside the appropriateness condition.

29. *I don't regret whether I saw him

Further conditions need to be specified for other cases, in particular:

a. the truth of the main clause is a matter of fact rather a matter of opinion
b. the truth (or otherwise) of the embedded proposition is specifiable at the time specified by the tense of the main verb

(In a more precise formulation (b) might well follow from (a) or vice versa.) <u>Feel</u> or <u>persuade</u> fall foul of (a), while <u>expect</u> falls foul of (b).

With complements beginning with a wh-word other than <u>whether</u> there is a further complicating factor. Such clauses can be interpreted as simple noun phrases in many instances, contrast, for instance:

30. I wonder what happened
31. I regret what happened

In (30), we have something more or less equivalent to a question ('What happened?'), but in (31) we know quite well what happened - the sentence can be paraphrased as 'I regret the thing that happened'. This type of sequence is often referred to as a 'free relative'. It is not altogether clear that there is a natural boundary between genuine embedded questions and free relatives. Contrast the following:

32. a. I wonder why he came
    b. I don't know why he came
    c. I understand why he came

(a) is a simple embedded question; (c) cannot be a straightforward embedded question, as <u>understand</u> does not naturally take such things:

33. *I understand whether he came

But (c) can be paraphrased as 'I understand the reason why he came'. With (b), both possibilities seem to exist, as <u>don't</u> <u>know</u> can take normal interrogative complements, but there is also the paraphrase 'I don't know the reason why he came'. It may therefore be that there is some sort of neutralisation of the difference between embedded interrogative and free relative.

EXERCISE 2

Look at a range of verbs in a variety of different forms (interrogative, negative, with modals, etc.) and examine the possibility of the occurrence of interrogative complements with <u>whether</u>, <u>what</u> and <u>why</u>. What refinements or changes to the pattern proposed here seem evident?

10.4. WHEN IS **THAT** OMISSIBLE?

<u>That</u>-clauses occur after a very large set of verbs (large, that is, relative to the size of the set of verbs which take sentence complements at all - this is really a fairly small set), and a large proportion of these occur also without the <u>that</u>:

34. a. He said that she was wrong
    b. He said she was wrong
35. a. He agreed that he had been wrong
    b. He agreed he had been wrong

There is a smallish class of verbs, however, which are very odd in the absence of <u>that</u>:

36. a. He whispered that she was wrong
    b. ??He whispered she was wrong
37. a. He wrote that he was feeling ill

172

    b. *He wrote he was feeling ill

It seems likely that intuitions differ quite considerably at this point; certainly mine differ from those of Alexander and Kunz, the first page of whose list of verbs occurring with that-complements I include as Table 10.1. Again, the asterisk is meant to indicate dubious cases, while the 'a' after an entry indicates that that is not omissible. I find many of their intuitions hard to accept - on the whole they are much more 'permissive' than me.

    There are certain cases where the omissibility of that is determined by syntactic context, possibly as a result of perceptual constraints on the form of sentences. This is most obvious in subject complements, where that is never omissible:

    38. a. That John is here must prove something

        b. *John is here must prove something

The nature of the perceptual principle that this might violate relates to the delimitation of main and subordinate clauses; we know that an object complement is going to be subordinate, whether or not it has a that, because we have already seen the main verb of the sentence, and therefore we will not find another main verb unless we are beginning a new sentence, or conjoining two sentences with the help of some such conjunction as and. With subject complements, on the other hand, the absence of a specific mark of subordination gives us no clue as to whether we are dealing with a main or subordinate clause. A sentence which starts John is here will be interpreted as having that sequence as its main clause; to find something else which could only be a main clause verb confuses the strategy that we have adopted for finding the main clause. This is a simple and natural principle having as its effect the exclusion of that-less subordinate clauses at the beginning of a sentence. It is clear, however, that it does not help us very much to decide when that should be omissible **after** a main verb.

    More relevant is the fact that some verbs appear to allow differences in meaning to be partially dependent on the omission of that:

    39. a. I understand that this is very complex

        b. I understand this is very complex

Understand is used in two different senses; one refers to processes of comprehension, while the other one has little independent semantic content, merely underlining that the information specified in the complement sentence is second-hand - it is not part of the speaker's personal experience but has been conveyed from some third person. In this sense,

TABLE 10.1   Verbs occurring with that-complements

*abide		cable		deduce	
accept	a	calculate		*delineate	
acknowledge	a	call to mind		demonstrate	
add		*can help		denote	a
adduce	a	can stand	a	deny	
adjudge	a	can tell		*depone	
admit		care	a	*depose	
*adumbrate		catch		*depreciate	
advertise		*cause		*descry	
*advise		caution		*deserve	
*advocate		certify		*designate	
*affect		*challenge		*desire	
affirm		charge		detect	
agree		check	a	determine	
allege		choose	a	*dictate	
allow		cite		disallow	a
announce		claim		disbelieve	a
*annunciate		*commence		discern	
answer		communicate		disclaim	
anticipate		complain		disclose	
appreciate		comprehend		discover	
apprehend		compute		*discuss	
argue		concede		*dislike	
*arrange		conceive		display	
*articulate		conclude		dispute	
ascertain		confess		*distinguish	
assert		confide		divine	
*assess		confirm		divulge	
assume		conjecture		document	
*augur		consider		doubt	
aver		*construe		*dread	
*avouch		*contemplate		dream	
*avow		contend		*echo	
bear in mind	a	contest	a	elaborate	
*begin		*continue		*elect	
*behold		contribute		elicit	a
believe		*controvert		emphasise	
bet		convey		*endure	
*bethink		*corroborate		*enjoy	
*betoken		*counsel		ensure	
*betray		count	a	entail	
boast		counterclaim		enter	a
*brag		*covenant		*enunciate	
*bring forth		*cry		envisage	
bring out		cry out	a	establish	
bring to light	a	decide		estimate	
bring up		declare		*evidence	
broadcast		decree		*exclude	

174

I *understand* means more or less the same as *apparently*. It seems to me that (39a) is somewhat biased in favour of the comprehension interpretation of *understand*, while (39b) is heavily biased towards - perhaps even exclusively reserved for - the meaning of lack of personal responsibility for the truth of the report.

There seems to be a wide variety of other features which are relevant to the choice between *that*-present and *that*-absent. The question of the category of element to which the clause is a complement is one such feature: clauses can be complements of nouns, of adjectives or of verbs:

40. The *fact* that he is coming (is odd)
41. I am *aware* that he is coming
42. I *suspect* that he is coming

I suggest that omission of *that* is much more likely after a verb than after an adjective or a noun. This is not to say that cases do not occur where a 'bare' complement occurs after a noun or an adjective, but rather that any comparison of their frequency of occurrence will show that such cases are excessively rare, in comparison with the highly frequent omission of *that* after verbs. It is incidentally interesting in this connection to look at the occurrence of such complements after passive participles, given the discussion of chapter 5 about their status as adjectival or verbal elements. Such scanty data as I have suggests that *that* is seldom omitted after a passive participle, but there are other factors which may be relevant here, and I have no firm conclusions to offer, in fact.

A second point of relevance is the question of the syntactic position of the complement clause. If there is something interposed between the verb and the complement clause, it is nearly always the case that *that* is retained:

43. I think quite honestly that he was joking
44. They suggested to her that she should go to court
45. I'm not certain really that it makes that much difference

This clearly relates in some degree to the use of *that* after passives, as the passive agent may occur between the participle and the complement sentence:

46. It has been claimed by Chomsky that languages are structure-dependent

The same thing appears to be true if the complement sentence contains a preposed adverbial clause or phrase:

47. I think that, if you look at it carefully,

you'll understand

48. I felt that, apart from that one passage, it was quite easy

Observations of spoken data occasionally come up with cases without <u>that</u>:

49. I remember when I studied philosophy we were confronted with a question ...

There is, of course, a difficulty in such cases in that it is not <u>a priori</u> obvious what the relevant syntactic structure should be. We can contrast two orthographically quite clear sentences:

50. Don't forget that if you get into trouble you can always phone

51. Don't forget: if you get into trouble you can always phone

The written form suggests that (50) is a single sentence involving a complement clause, while (51) is really two separate sentences, the second of which clarifies the first. It is not altogether clear how such alternatives can be resolved in spoken English, although the two possibilities are still there. Certainly there may be cases where the intonation makes everything relatively explicit; but intonation is by no means a reliable guide. Very deliberate delivery may involve pausing before <u>that</u>; in normal speech, however, quite distinct sentences may be run on in a single intonational contour.

A third factor which appears to be of relevance is the frequency of the verb which takes the complement: certain verbs, such as <u>say</u>, <u>think</u> and <u>believe</u>, account for a disproportionate quantity of <u>that</u>-less complements. There is a fairly restricted set of verbs, it seems, where we intuitively feel that the complement must have <u>that</u>: but the vast majority of verbs **typically** occur with <u>that</u>, even though there is no logical necessity in this. Spoken data that I have looked at have well over half their object complements without <u>that</u>, but the set of distinct verbs which occur more than once or twice in such use is very restricted indeed.

Tempo, colloquial status, etc. are further factors which are clearly relevant here: <u>that</u>-omission is acceptable in many places, but tends to occur in more colloquial, more rapidly delivered, speech. I have not attempted to make any comparative study of this, but it is not altogether improbable that there is a natural relationship between this feature and the verb-frequency feature. The point here is that most uses of <u>say</u>, <u>think</u>, <u>believe</u>, etc. are semi-redundant in their normal use in speech, and are therefore likely to be delivered at a fairly rapid rate. We would expect all sorts of factors about sentence accent to be relevant here as well.

10.5. ON THE VARIABLE OCCURRENCE OF **THAT**

I have discussed a number of factors which are conducive to either the omission or the retention of that in finite complement clauses. In many of the grammatical alternations discussed at various points throughout this book, it has at least appeared plausible that factors of some linguistically-specifiable type provide a context requiring the use of one set of forms, and other factors require the alternate forms - i.e. such alternations appear to be linguistically determinate, to yield to an account solely in terms of grammatical factors. But the presence or absence of that is not such a factor: even a high-frequency verb followed immediately by a complement sentence may include that - there is nothing odd about a sentence such as (52):

52. He said that he was coming

A traditional grammarian would perhaps have invoked 'style' at this point, where purely grammatical criteria break down. A slightly more refined version of this demarche comes from modern sociolinguistics, with the notion of 'sociolinguistic variable'. There is a large and rapidly-growing literature on such an approach, and a whole range of attitudes to its validity and appropriate place within linguistics. From the point of view of this book, the essential thing about it is its attempt to correlate alternations with such factors as social class, age, sex, level of formality, etc. The major distinctive feature which this work has is the fact that an attempt is made to show these factors at work in terms of quantitative studies of their occurrence in texts. It turns out that no hard-and-fast rules emerge from such studies, but that there are consistent regularities relating to **proportions** of uses of forms. For example, studies of the use of the alternation (n)-(ng) ([ŋ]) in progressive forms of the verb in English show that virtually all speakers use both forms, but higher social class correlates with a higher proportion of (ng) - except in the huntin', shootin' and fishin' set - as does more formal style, and so on. These correlations are extremely consistent; it remains a mystery what mechanisms of variation allow speakers to 'compute' the appropriate number of forms to use in a given situation.

It is clearly possible in principle to apply such methods to the use or omission of <u>that</u> in finite complements. It would probably be a major piece of research to do this over some linguistic community; there has to be a good number of examples for each level of formality and each class of speakers, and the corpus required to test this to a level which might yield significant results would be astronomically large. One of the reasons why phonological features have been a major subject of sociolinguistic studies is that a given phonological phenomenon is likely to recur with much greater frequency in a given text than a given syntactic phenomenon. Any spoken text contains many more phonological units than it does syntactic units, by definition.

It is, however, possible to produce something which is a pale reflection of such a study by looking at texts which might be expected to reproduce some part of some such variation. As a modest attempt at such a pilot study, I looked at the occurrence of <u>that</u> in three British national newspapers, the **Sun**, the **Daily Mail** and the **Daily Telegraph** (henceforth S, M and T). These newspapers are ordered here in what is generally said to be a progression of 'seriousness'; ideologically, however, there are few differences between them, and this can therefore be excluded as a factor in variation. This gradation in 'seriousness' is reflected quite simply in the amount of text they contain; I only managed to find 79 finite complements in an issue of S, while I took the first 100 examples from M and T - which in the case of T covered less than half of the text in the newspaper. **Sun**-readers tend to prefer pictures. It would be possible to interpret the differences between these newspapers as representing either social class or gradations of formality of style, S being lowest-class/least formal, and T being highest-class/most formal. As there is usually some sort of correlation between these factors anyway, either interpretation would make sense from the point of view of linguistic variation.

Table 10.2 shows some of the figures associated with these texts. If we claim that the sequence S - M - T represents the low-high continuum, the results are roughly as expected. S has by far the largest proportion of <u>that</u>-omission, T the least. One might wish to put these down as consequences of some other pattern of variation in these newspapers; but separation of verb and its complement, number of noun and adjectives as governors of complement clauses, and range of verbs used do not differ sufficiently to account for these differences. The choice of verbs used in these newspapers is not without interest; T has by far the highest proportion of uses of <u>say</u>, most of which are <u>that</u>-less, but this still leaves T with the lowest proportion of omission of <u>that</u>. The use of other verbs is also interesting: S and M make quite frequent use of <u>know</u> and <u>think</u> (5-6 uses of each in each newspaper) but these are not used at all in T. T in turn makes much greater use of verbs like <u>indicate</u> and <u>note</u>. There seems, therefore, to be a contrast of private and public verbs between the more 'popular' newspapers and the 'newspaper of record'. However, I have no data which would suggest that this particular distinction is relevant to the presence or otherwise of <u>that</u>.

Table 10.2. The occurrence of finite non-interrog-
ative complement sentences in one issue of three
British national newspapers.

(%)	Sun(79)	Mail(100)	Telegraph(100)
without that	58	40	31
V and S separated	24	24	20
occurrence of that with V and S separated	84	79	85
occurrence of that after nouns (number of instances in brackets)	100 (5)	100 (11)	100 (9)
occurrence of that after adjectives (number of instances in brackets)	50 (2!)	0 (5)	100 (5)
occurrence of say as governor	11	12	31
occurrence of that after say	0	33	25
number of distinct verbal lexemes as governors	35	38	36

READING - CHAPTER 10

The perceptual basis for the non-omissibility of
that in subject complements was first proposed by T.
Bever in 'The cognitive basis for linguistic
structures', J. Hayes (ed) Cognition and the
Development of Language. On direct questions see R.
A. Hudson 'The meaning of questions', Language 51,
1-31, 1975. For some historical data on omission of

that in English, see A. Warner Complementation in Middle English and the Methodology of Historical Syntax, London: Croom Helm, 1982, pp168-77.

A good account of sociolinguistic variation with the progressive is B. Wald and T. Shopen 'A researcher's guide to the sociolinguistic variable (ING)', T. Shopen and J. M. Williams (eds) Style and Variables in English, Cambridge, Mass.: Winthrop, 1981, pp250-68.

Chapter Eleven

CONCLUSION

In the course of this book questions of classification - usually though not always semantic - have
arisen constantly. All but the most boring aspects
of verbal behaviour in English are restricted in
some way, and the division of verbs into subclasses
is normally necessary to provide an account of the
ways in which various types of behaviour are
restricted. In the transitivity chapter alone there
are many subclasses of verbs mentioned, and the
semantic properties of these verbs play a major role
in their behaviour, if not an exclusive one (cf. the
apparent role of frequency in 'ergative' verbs for a
non-semantic criterion).
    However, even on the assumption that the
solutions proposed here are more or less correct
(which is a fairly unrealistic assumption) the use
of ad hoc features, based on an inductive procedure
of generalising from some set of English data, is
likely to end up with no very coherent set of
principles which might account for the systematic
patterning of the meaning and grammatical behaviour
of English verbs. It seems that we are caught
between the Scylla of factual inadequacy and the
Charybdis of theoretical triviality. On the one hand
there is the sort of classification which case
grammar promises (although it fails to deliver, on
the whole), whereby significant semantic **and** syntactic features will follow semi-automatically from the
'case frame' of verbs - the position that there is
actually some relatively simple way of predicting
which verbs occur with which case labels on the
basis of the meaning of verbs, and that other properties of sentences will follow from the set of case
labels they contain. On the other hand we have a set
of heterogeneous features such as those proposed
throughout this book or - to cite a more respectable

source - the classification of English verbs provided by Leech in various places (including GCE); the choice of these features is justified to a considerable degree by the facts which they have individually been chosen to reflect, and yet the whole classification does not hang together as forming a system of any sort, as a rational partition of verb types.

Clearly both theory-internal justification and descriptive motivation are necessary for us to have any sort of complete satisfaction - but both types are also heavily dependent on factors which change with time; there is a particularly high turnover of theoretical positions at the moment, and the choice of one or other theoretical position is likely to entail a different starting point for a rational classification of verbs. On the other hand, the use of inductive methods will change every time particular constructions are reanalysed in various ways, and it is likely that different semantic features will be induced from different analyses. When it is taken into account that even something as well known and heavily researched as aspect in English is a matter of great controversy, it will not be surprising if quite distinct bases for classification proliferate. Indeed there are studies (particularly of French) which suggest very strongly that there are very large numbers of distinct ways of classifying verbs, all based on their grammatical behaviour.

11.2. LINGUISTIC CLASSIFICATIONS

As I have mentioned at various points, one of the products of case grammar has been a classification of verbs. The basic intuition of case grammar is that verbs characterise the noun phrases which they occur with in terms of semantic labels such as 'Agent' (the performer, initiator, causer of the action), 'Experiencer' (the being experiencing the action/emotion), 'Object' (or 'patient' - the neutral participant in the action). The 'case frame' is the set of semantic labels which a verb typically imposes on the noun phrases which occur with it; verbs can then be categorised in terms of their case frames. Curiously enough, nobody has pursued such a classification in any systematic way - in the sense of trying to use the notion of case frames as a **generator** of verb types. The sort of thing which might result from such an attempt is this: if we limit ourselves to the three 'major' syntactically

relevant cases - O(bjective), A(gent) and E(xperi-
encer) and list verbs which can be associated with
any given set of cases in particular sentences:
O - stand, exist, go, arrive, etc.
A - speak, lie, smile, etc.
O A - break, read, eat, kill, etc.
E - be warm, relax, etc.
O E - like, enjoy, see, etc.
A E - surprise, disappoint, hurt, etc.
O A E - administer?
    This list would be interpreted as saying that
these verbs occur in contexts where there is exactly
one noun phrase for each element of their case
frame. Of course some verbs occur in more than one
case frame, and it might further be useful to compare classes of verbs in terms of the range of
distinct case frames they occur in (cf. Fillmore's
use of brackets to indicate the range of case frames
that a verb co-occurs with). There will be semantic
features which follow from the case frames (fairly
circularly, given that the cases are semantically
defined) - e.g. any frame with E in it will refer to
some sort of psychological state in one participant.
It is generally hoped that such distinctions as
'state' vs 'action', or whatever, will follow from
this classification without having to be specified,
but the detailed basis of this is not clear, partly
because the assignment of case frames has varied
over the period of case grammar's existence. An
example is the treatment of a verb like hit, which
was analysed as having a Locative object in one of
Fillmore's better known articles, but which has been
treated as a 'normal', O-object verb in treatments
since then.
    I have already pointed out (chapter 2.6) that
case grammar only works really nicely over a relatively restricted range of verbs. This is not to say
that no version of case grammar can be constructed
to provide an adequate account of verb classes in
general, but merely that the intuitive procedures
normally accepted within case grammar of assigning
verbs to particular case frames break down fairly
quickly given a reasonable range of types of verb.
It is surprising that case grammarians have not
investigated the combinatorial possibilities of case
labels systematically, because such a procedure
might hold out some hope of motivating the assignment of case frames to verbs in ways other than
intuitive semantic characterisations. If we agree
with the early line that the object of hit is a
Locative case NP, then we are entitled to ask how

the Locative case will combine - say - with the Experiencer case. It might not be altogether implausible to claim that the verb see is one which has an Experiencer subject and Locative object, given such sentences as:
1. I can see into the room
2. Superman can see through brick walls
Most case grammarians would claim that see has the case frame [O E], as suggested in the previous paragraph, but the alternative suggestion of [E L], based largely on what might otherwise be a combinatorial gap, has some plausibility, and would suffice to distinguish a class of verbs of perception from verbs of cognitive or emotional state.

Such speculations interact closely with the question of how individual cases may be defined semantically. If we accept that the objects of simple transitive verbs may be in any one of a whole range of cases, then we are more likely to be able to define the Objective case in terms of some positive semantic features - e.g. that it marks participants **affected** by the action of the verb. It is notable from the discussions of previous chapters of this book - especially of chapters 2 and 4 - that the notion of affected object has some role to play in determining the syntactic behaviour of English verbs. If this is accepted, then it would seem that whichever semantic categorisation of English verbs is to be used has to provide room for the notion of 'affected object'.

Three things follow from this discussion. Firstly, case grammar is flexible enough to be capable of modification in line with the sorts of analysis which have been put forward in this book. Secondly, however, no currently proposed version of case grammar provides an adequate account of English verbs from the present perspective. Thirdly, although case grammar is clearly a pleasing **notation**, the empirical claim lurking within it - that the semantic properties of verbs determine the syntactic environments they occur in - looks rather more dubious, given that semantic criteria alone prove virtually useless in determining possible case frames. There are many syntactically irrelevant semantic properties; the classes of case grammar are essentially determined on purely syntactic grounds.

Other linguistic classifications of verbs have tended on the whole to be purely ad hoc, just as they have been in this book. In other words, a set of phenomena have been shown to work only for one set of verbs, and then the common semantic content of this set of verbs is given. There is nothing wrong with this procedure, of course, but it is an exercise which can be repeated in very different ways, and the status of such typologies is not altogether secure. GCE, for instance, basing itself largely on the work of Geoffrey Leech, divides verbs for the purposes of tense and aspect into Dynamic and Stative; Dynamic verbs divide into activity, process, bodily sensation, transitional event and momentary verbs, while Stative verbs divide into verbs of inert perception and cognition, and re-lational verbs. As a classification this is both fairly clear and reasonably adequate for its purposes. Indeed, it shows promise as a classific-ation which may be extended to other areas; thus, for instance, the class of 'relational' verbs in-cludes many of those which do not have a passive form in English. But the **semantic** status of this class is far from clear - the following verbs, among others, are cited as being in this class:

> possess, remain (a bachelor), require, resemble, seem, sound, suffice.

What is 'relational' about <u>sound</u>, for instance? It is clear what these verbs have in common - lack of a progressive form; but the quasi-semantic label is in that case merely an excuse for not giving an exhaustive listing of these verbs. Note incidentally that some of these verbs sound perfectly reasonable with the progressive:

> 3. a. I'm remaining a bachelor if I can help it
>   b. He was seeming a bit off colour when I
>   last saw him
>   c. It's sounding good

The criticisms I have made of these semantic classifications do not affect the point that some of the linguistic analysis that lies at the basis of these classifications is intelligent and helpful. But the semantic labels used are essentially a <u>post hoc</u> exercise designed, I suspect, for convenience of nomenclature, rather than as helpful components of a semantic theory. Of course semantic theory needs to be justified in terms of the variable behaviour of semantically distinct elements in grammar; but we have seen - most notably in the discussion of tense in chapter 1 - that there may be many semantic characterisations which at least approximately reflect the co-occurrence of verbs and grammatical categories. It is unlikely that purely grammatical investigations will allow us to choose between alternatives.

11.3. ACTIVITIES, ACCOMPLISHMENTS AND ACHIEVEMENTS

If we cannot find an appropriate semantic framework within linguistics, it might seem to make sense to look outside linguistics - the philosophical literature being an obvious place to look. One classification which many linguists have now taken up is that of Vendler (although elements of this classification date from Aristotle at least). This classification is based on a number of distinct types of evidence - from semantic entailments which occur in relation to specific linguistic forms, from co-occurrence evidence with adverbials, other verbs, etc., and from the occurrence of verbs in particular grammatical forms. One entailment criterion, for instance, distinguishes verbs where the following holds:

4. If NP Vs for a certain period, then NP Vs at any point within that period.

E.g., sentences (5) and (6) have this property, but (7) does not:

5. For three years I believed that I had been cheated
6. He ran for three hours
7. He dug a hole for three hours

If I believed something for three years, then I believed it at every point during those three years; in fact our use of language is flexible enough to allow for a few moments of doubt, but something close to this has to be true. But if I dug a hole for three hours, it does not follow that I dug a hole at every point during those three hours. Co-occurrence criteria include, for instance, the use of manner adverbials such as <u>carefully</u> with verbs, distinguishing the following sentences:

8. He carefully ran round the puddle
9. He carefully dug a hole in his lawn
10. *He carefully believed he had been cheated
11. *He carefully recognised his sister in the crowd

Grammatical criteria include, for instance, the naturalness of imperative sentences:

12. Run round the puddle
13. Dig a hole in the lawn
14. *Believe that you have been cheated
15. *Recognise me

The conclusion of such tests is that it is possible to distinguish four classes in terms of consistent behaviour - activities, accomplishments, states and achievements, corresponding to the verbs in (12)-

(15) respectively. 'State' and 'activity' more or less correspond to their everyday senses - both may continue indefinitely. 'Accomplishments' are inherently circumscribed activities, while 'achievements' have been termed 'lucky accomplishments' - it is as appropriate to say that they happen to you as that you perform them. In fact, of course, what is being categorised here is not verbs as such, but rather verb phrases - dig (as an intransitive verb phrase) is different in its behaviour from dig a hole.

There are two points here which give rise to a certain amount of doubt about aspects of this classification. Firstly, it is based on criteria which are not substantially different from those which have motivated (or failed to motivate) the linguistic analyses that we have seen. There has always been a strong element of linguistic analysis in philosophy, and it is essentially the grammatical behaviour of these verbs which seems to give rise to this classification. There is nothing wrong with this, as I have already suggested in the last section, but it does mean that any possibility that such classifications should be independently justified from some other source looks rather more remote. The second point is that the intuitive content of these labels, while partially reminiscent of traditional labels, is not altogether clear: it is not the case that the distinctions made between these four categories of predicate types are automatically recognisable by any speaker of English, or even by any linguist. The assignment of a verb to a class is a function of its behaviour according to the criteria; i.e. the verb classes do not exist independently of the criteria, they do not have sufficient semantic clarity to jump free of their syntactic correlates.

The Vendler classification is a good one - it has been used by philosophers and linguists and refined in certain ways, but the basic framework of analysis has remained remarkably constant. But as soon as we start looking at verb classes in more linguistic depth, this classification will be testable just as any other linguistically-based classification is - it has no privileged position which insulates it from its purely linguistic basis.

11.4. THE ROLE OF SEMANTIC CLASSIFICATIONS

The work done in this book might be relevant in two distinct ways to the question of an appropriate

Conclusion

semantic classification of English verbs. Firstly, much attention has been given to the possibility of adopting different semantic (or indeed other) hypotheses for the same data, and there is a fair amount of detailed comparison of such hypotheses. Secondly, an attempt is made in this book to look at a fairly wide range of grammatical phenomena centring round the verb in English, and as such, it gives a rather wider range of data to be considered in evaluating different classifications. On the other hand, there are two further factors which indicate that there may be great problems in establishing such a classification. The discussion of chapter 1 in particular seems to suggest that there may be alternative possibilities of correlation which are all reasonable within some degree of error, which might be eliminated by considerations of markedness, or pragmatic interpretation, or whatever. In other words, if the tense-aspect discussion proved typical, there might be no way in which a well-justified evaluation of alternatives could be carried out. Secondly, even assuming that it is possible to make a clear-cut distinction in such cases, it has also turned out that the subtlety and detail of semantic categorisations has no manifest upper limit - at least if some of the discussions in this book are reasonable. For instance, in considering ergative uses of verbs in chapter 2, it appeared relevant to make a distinction between verbs like cut and verbs like break, along the lines that the latter refers exclusively to result, while the former refers to both process and result. Some such distinctions appear to be necessary, but given that none of the analyses presented in this book have **totally** exhausted the set of verbs which do or do not behave in a certain way, there are likely to be further features which will be relevant, and (on the assumption that I have not missed many obvious analyses) these are likely to be more subtle.

What conclusions can be drawn, then, from the overall structure of this book? We might start by enumerating the individual features shown to be relevant (where the numbers reflect the chapter in which that semantic category was found useful).

1. a. transition from one state to another
   b. instantaneous action with no necessary result
   c. state
2. a. object-affecting verbs
   b. object-creating verbs

Conclusion

     c. change of physical/mental state or
         location
     d. verbs of action <u>and</u> result
     e. result verbs with no action specified
     f. agent +/- presupposed
     g. actions
     h. subject-oriented vs. object-oriented
     i. action of the verb requires an object
  6. a. resultative
     b. action with a natural limit (telic)
  9. a. factive

Discussions of the type I have indulged in are not necessarily amenable to systematisation or simple naming in this way. Further semantic properties are certainly relevant to the areas I have discussed.

There appear to be two quite distinct types of phenomenon here in relation to the correlation of semantic class and grammatical behaviour. It is a fact about phrasal verbs in English, for instance, that they express resultative meaning. A class of verb phrases with no natural specifiable limit will therefore tend not to combine with a grammatical construction of resultative meaning. There is an incompatibility here - the combination is not **grammatically** deviant, it is simply uninterpretable. By contrast, it is hard to see the lack of <u>that</u>-complements after <u>want</u> as anything other than a fact which needs to be stated as a lexical property of <u>want</u>. More generally, whatever criteria there may be which partially determine the class of verbs nominalising with the suffix <u>-ation</u>, it is impossible to see lack of a nominal form as being the result of some semantic or pragmatic incompatibility - i.e. it is purely a **grammatical** or **lexical** fact about <u>condemn</u> that it occurs with -ation while <u>annoy</u> does not.

There is a complicating factor here. If a grammatical pattern is **very** regular, then it may well overflow its natural limits, the problem of incompatibility of interpretation being solved by a (conventionalised?) change of meaning of the whole construction. Thus the progressive aspect (which - let us accept - has imperfective meaning) is odd in many contexts with stative verbs like <u>understand</u>, <u>know</u> and <u>think</u>. But such forms do occur, as in (16):

  16. a. I'm understanding trace theory at last
     b. ?I'm knowing more of the answers these
        days
     c. I'm thinking that it wasn't such a good
        idea after all

There seems to be a suggestion of 'development' in

(a) and (b), and of 'passing thought' in (c). All would be incompatible with the 'stative' meaning which suggests an invariable constancy. So the general semantic incompatibility of the progressive with these verbs is absent when they are used in a different sense. It is not the meaning of the grammatical form which is altered, but rather the lexical meaning of the verb.

This distinction – of compatibility conditioned by interpretability, as opposed to that conditioned in a relatively arbitrary fashion – raises the interesting question how the phenomena enumerated above distribute among these types. It seems at least possible that many of the phenomena we have considered involve (in)compatibility of the meaning of the construction with that of the verb (phrase). If this is so, then the question of verb classification immediately becomes less acute. The fact that a construction is selective automatically partitions the elements it selects from. But any given partitioning of the set of verbs does not necessarily correspond to a **single** semantic feature. There could be many specific features, just as the progressive, for instance, may imply that something is incomplete by virtue of it being only partially done (17a), or by virtue of it having no natural end point (17b), or by virtue of it being repeated and further repeatable (17c):

17. a. He is writing an essay
    b. He is walking
    c. He is banging on the door

It is perhaps perverse to try to claim that these represent a single aspect of meaning simply because the progressive can be interpreted as imperfective with all of them.

The discussion of previous chapters can therefore be reinterpreted. I have tended to talk as if it is necessary to have a semantic categorisation of verbs directly reflecting their grammatical behaviour. If we reject that interpretation then what I have done instead is to make a set of proposals as to what meaning some specific constructions have. The set of verbs that go with these constructions is then a matter of the speaker deciding whether something conveys the intended message. Intended messages will typically make some sense. This reinterpretation will not leave a significantly smaller number of constructions unaccounted for. But it may leave us feeling less guilty about the arbitrariness of our semantic classifications.

Such an interpretation has in fact seemed to be

at the basis of many of the analyses espoused (tentatively) in previous chapters. For instance, the analysis of the pseudo-intransitive construction in chapter 2 was based on the possibility of interpreting the 'derived' subject as representing something which could exert an influence on the action specified by the verb. Such a characterisation is all too vague, but it is clear that it makes little sense to look on such an analysis as representing some sort of subclassification of **verbs** in general: there is no more reason to expect that a rational semantic classification of verbs will involve the possibility of their objects having an influence on the action specified by them than there is of verbs being categorised in terms of the possibility of their actions being associated with the use of screwdrivers. One of the reasons why it is so difficult to make exceptionless generalisations in the case of pseudo-intransitive verbs is that the acceptability of the construction depends on the possibility of there being a particular sort of interpretation. Such a possibility is to a large extent dependent on non-semantic factors (the ingenuity of hearers in constructing situations, the sort of situations which typically occur, etc.). The difference between pseudo-intransitive and ergative verbs in particular is that the latter are to a large degree **lexicalised**; while pseudo-intransitives can be assumed to be formed whenever the situation arises and the conditions are appropriate, the intransitive use of ergative verbs is necessarily represented in the idiosyncratic information which needs to be stored in relation to that verb (although of course there **are** general properties which characterise ergative verbs).

At this sort of point the goals of descriptive and theoretical grammar diverge: a theoretical account of pseudo-intransitives, for instance, will specify that such constructions are possible, but, if my informal observations are at all on the right lines, will not pose any grammatical restrictions on the construction, but simply state that the constraints which apply depend on pragmatic factors of various sorts, which are not to be construed as part of a grammatical description of English. A descriptive account, on the other hand, needs to specify the various conditions on the use of these grammatical forms, to show what is normal and what is abnormal, what is typical and what a deviation from this. It will not help a learner, or a machine, or any interested person, if we tell them that

Conclusion

pseudo-intransitive constructions occur freely (as far as the grammarian is concerned), but that there are restrictions which an as yet unwritten pragmatics of English will throw light on.

READING - CHAPTER 11

On the multiplicity of linguistic classifications see M. Gross Méthodes en syntaxe, Paris: Hermann, 1976. For case grammar, the references of chapter 2 apply again, while for Leech's classification GCE uses it, while it is given in more detailed form in G. Leech Meaning and the English Verb, London: Longman, 1969. Vendler's classification is presented in 'Verbs and times' Philosophical Review 56: 143-60 (1957), and in Z. Vendler Linguistics and Philosophy, Cornell, 1966. The best integration of this into other linguistic approaches is that of D. Dowty Word Meaning and Montague Grammar Dordrecht: Reidel, 1979. Problems of semantic classification, including much in relation to verbs, come in S. Pulman Word Meaning and Belief, London: Croom Helm, 1983.

INDEX

Index